Copyright Statement:

This book, along with all Test Prep Wizards materials, is protected by copyright. This book is for individual use only; under no circumstances may it be distributed, published, or licensed by any means without written consent of Test Prep Wizards.

Ownership of Trademarks

KTP Enterprises, LLC is the owner of the trademark "Test Prep Wizards" and the pictured Test Prep Wizards logos as well as the other marks that the Company may seek to use and protect from time to time in the ordinary course of business.

ACT is a trademark of ACT, Inc.

Screenshots were taken from the TI-SmartView CE Emulator Software and TI Connect CE software.

All other trademarks referenced are the property of their respective owners.

Publisher Name and Address:

Test Prep Wizards
268 Post Road,
Fairfield CT 06824

www.TestPrepWizards.com

Disclaimers:

The content provided herein is solely for educational purposes. Every effort has been made to ensure that the content provided in this eBook is accurate and helpful for readers at publishing time. However, this is not an exhaustive treatment of the subjects. No liability is assumed for losses or damages due to the information provided.

First Edition

www.TestPrepWizards.com

This page is intentionally left blank

A WORD FROM THE AUTHOR

Heya students,

I wrote this manual because I felt that there were no easy-to-read and follow books for using the Texas Instruments calculator. From my experience, the TI-84 is the one most used by the students with whom I work, so I figured, "If I write this, I can give it to students so that I don't have to waste instructional time going over calculator hacks with them!" The truth of that statement remains to be seen.

The goal of this manual was not to explain the absolute basics (Here's how to add—aren't you AMAZED!) but rather to explain some of the functions that most students, in my experience, do not know exist on the calculator.

I'd also like to say that, as a math professor and test preparation savant, using the calculator well does not replace conceptual flaws of the student. I hope that by outlining some of the lesser-known calculator skills, it will allow students to:

A. Grab a few more questions on the test with technology.
B. Allow for methods to check and ensure correct answers.

Additionally, one of the "problems" with calculator usage is that students *kinda* remember there's this way to do that thing on the calculator, but can't remember how and spend far too long hitting random buttons searching for something that looks like what they want. The only way to get become a calculator wizard is to practice—ideally randomly. You're not going to see 10 matrix questions in a row on the test, so once you've built up familiarity with a concept—in this case, solving with a calculator—you should have a friend, loved one, enemy, or whoever ask you how to do concepts from this manual at random. If you can nail it, you're building long-term mastery. Can't remember? Go back and review!

I tried to include as much as I could and have rock stars (not literal rock stars) go through and suggest edits. A truly huge shout out to Lindsay Channing-Larusso for her eagle eyes and patience with my lack of colons. Alas, mistakes may exist; sadly, I am only human. Any mistakes that creep into here are mine and mine alone. If you find something that is off, please do not hesitate to email me at Vinny@TestPrepWizards.com.

Another huge shout out to Sammie Zemanek for her work on the cover.

Feel like dropping me a message to say how life-changing this book is? Use the same email—I love hearing from happy folk!

Best of luck on the ACT!

Vinny Madera,
Founder—Test Prep Wizards

www.TestPrepWizards.com

TABLE OF CONTENTS

www.TestPrepWizards.com

NOTATION I USE

Some options on the calculator require you to press buttons in a certain order or require you to press a button that brings up a menu which will need to be navigated.

When you need to press multiple buttons, I'll write it like this:

For example, if you should press the blue 2ⁿᵈ button and then the comma button (that's how you can do scientific notation), I'd write it like this:

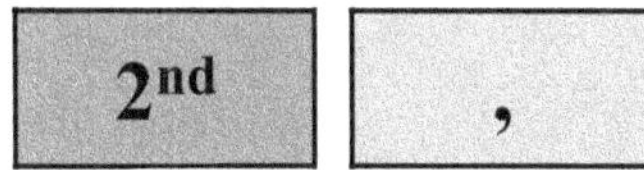

I'll try to match up the colors on the buttons as well. If the use is pretty straightforward, I'll also write buttons like this button in text. Many times, I will not show separate buttons when the meaning is clear. For instance, to write the number -7, you'd use two separate keys

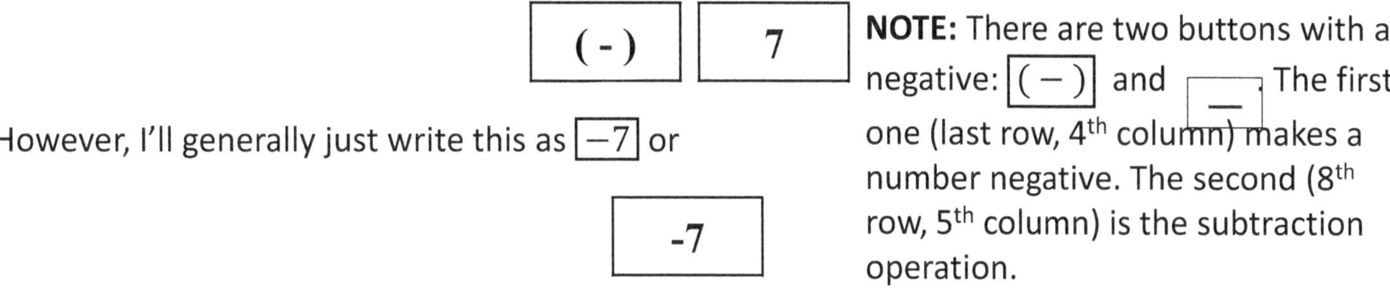

However, I'll generally just write this as -7 or

NOTE: There are two buttons with a negative: $(-)$ and ▭ The first one (last row, 4th column) makes a number negative. The second (8th row, 5th column) is the subtraction operation.

If pressing a button brings you to a menu, I'll show it this way:

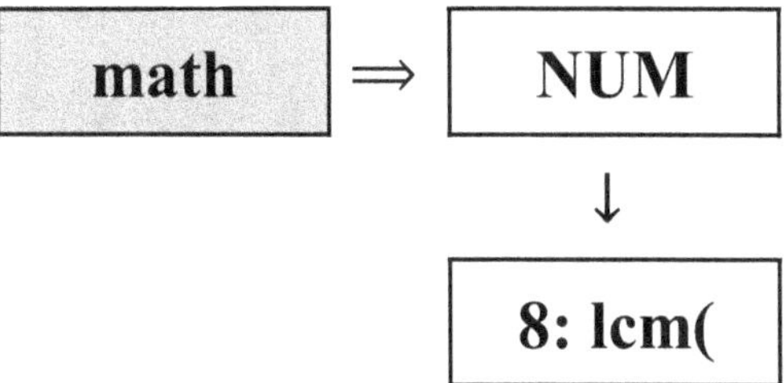

Here, you would press the math button, then press the right arrow to go to the NUM heading, and then down to the option listed. You can also press the number (or letter) to go directly to that option. In the above example, that would let you find the least common multiple of two numbers.

NOTATION I USE

Sometimes, I'll show an entire problem written out:

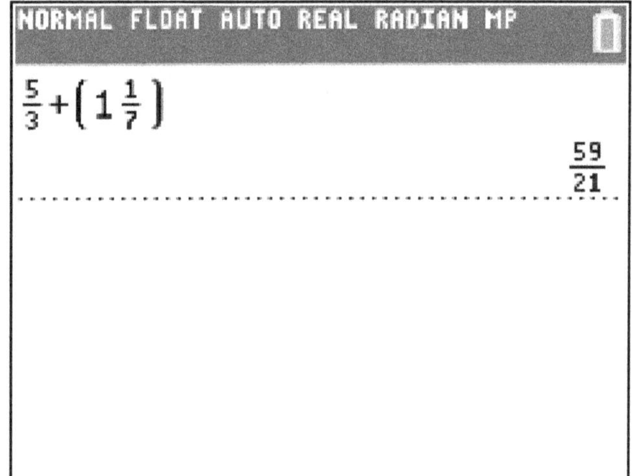

And provide the key history of what was typed:

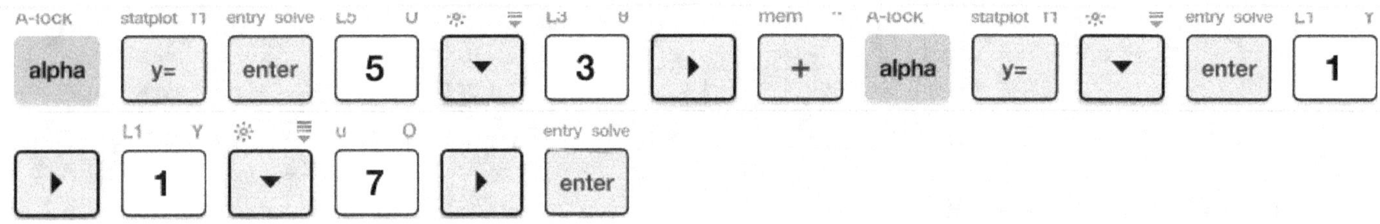

I anticipate that the key history will be easy enough to follow.

Sometimes, there are multiple ways to accomplish the same task. For instance, the addition of the fractions shown above could be accomplished with either of the following:

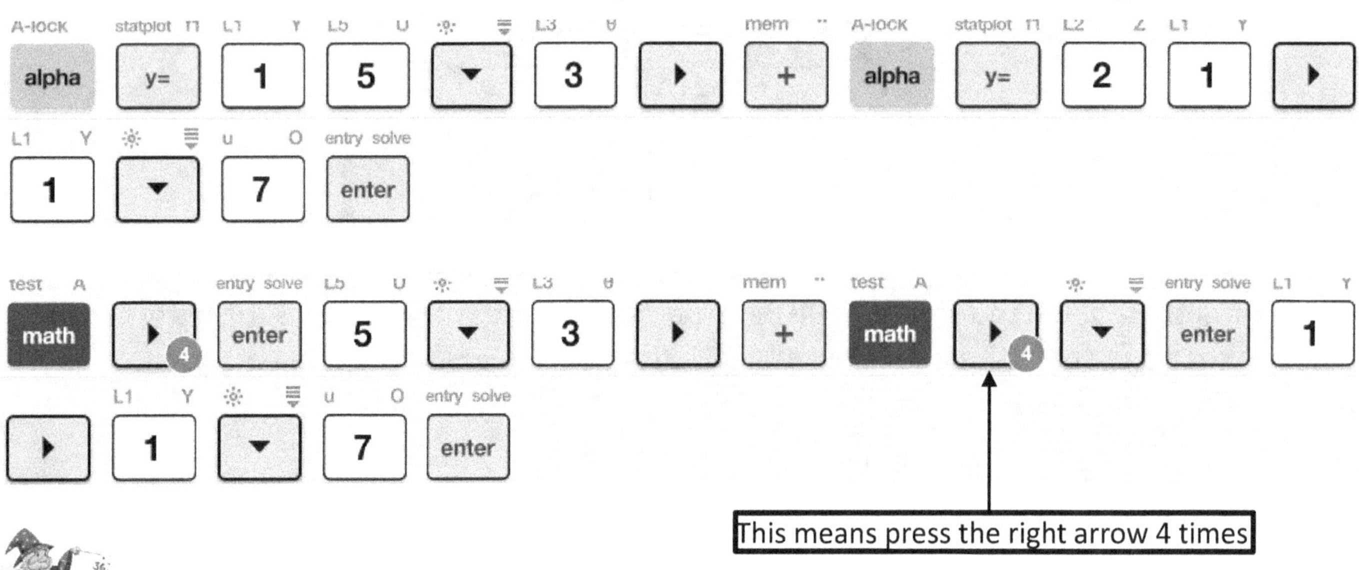

NOTATION I USE

Some functions on the calculator have **required arguments** and **optional arguments**. As you might imagine, the former are needed and the latter are not. To display what you need to input into the calculator, I'll write things this way:

calculatorFunction(Required Argument 1, Required Argument 2, … , [Optional Arguments])

Arguments usually take on values like numbers, but they can also be variables. Arguments, both required and optional, get separated by commas—located one button above the 7.

Most TI-84 plus calculators come equipped with the Catalog Help option already enabled. This allows you to bring up the required and optional arguments for many functions.

To access the help feature in a menu, scroll down to the function in a menu and press the +. That will bring up the necessary arguments for that function.

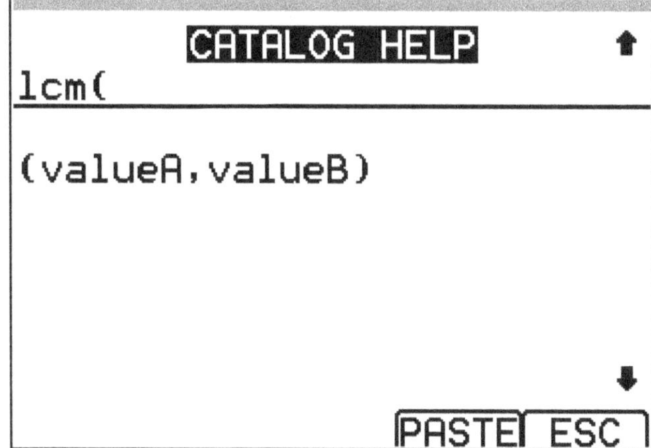

You can see that that after pressing the +, there are two required arguments for a least common multiple—namely the two numbers that you are looking to take a least common multiple of.

NOTE: Some calculators do not have Catalog Help on by default. To turn it on, you'll need to access it through apps. Press apps, scroll down to CtlgHelp, and press enter.

SECOND NOTE: Some calculators do not have have Catalog Help on by default or preloaded. You can always download it from the Texas Instruments website. See the apps appendix for a how-to.

INITIAL SETUP

There are some options that you will want to turn on, or make sure are turned on, on your calculator. Press the mode and make sure the following options are highlighted. In case one of the options listed below is not highlighted, just scroll down to the particular option and press enter.

NOTE: Some of the screens in this workbook may look different than what is on your screen. This may be due to the MATHPRINT vs. CLASSIC option. *I highly recommend* the MATHPRINT option.

SOME KEY (no pun intended) BUTTONS

There are three different options for most buttons on the calculator.

1. **Primary options.** This is generally what the button says. Many are common sense. for instance, x^2 squares whatever you just typed. Some buttons are important but are not necessarily intuitive. For example, sto → will store whatever you just typed in as a variable. This is a very important button!

2. **Secondary options.** These options are accessed by pressing the 2nd button (second row, first column). Pressing this button and then another button will access whatever is written in blue above a button. More on that in a sec.

3. **Third options.** These options are accessed by pressing the alpha button (third row, first column). Pressing this button and then another button will access whatever is written in green above a button.

EXAMPLE: The decimal button (last row, third column).

Primary option—inserting a decimal point in a number.
Secondary option—inserting the imaginary number, i.
Third option—inserting a colon (used to separate expressions)

THE SECRET MENU

The TI-84 plus and later editions contain a shortcut menu used with the top row of buttons (graphing buttons) that many students and dinosaur teachers do not know about. To access it, press any of the following combinations:

Fraction Menu	**alpha**	y =
Function Menu	**alpha**	window
Matrix Menu	**alpha**	zoom
y Variables Menu	**alpha**	trace

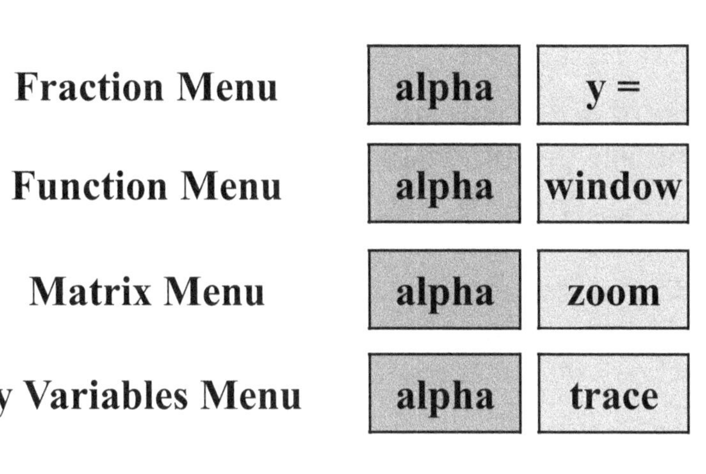

This will bring up screens that look like the following:

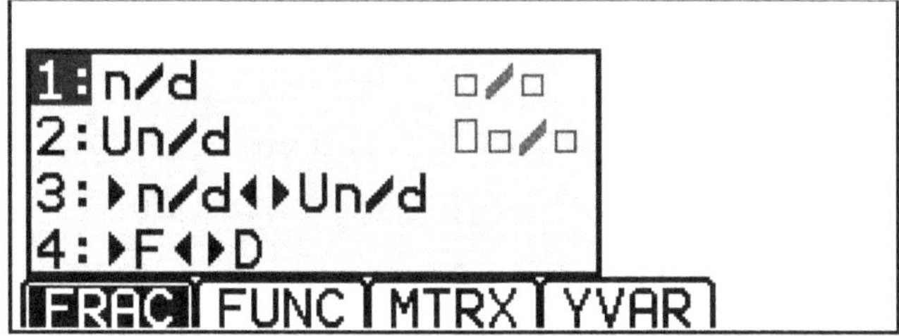

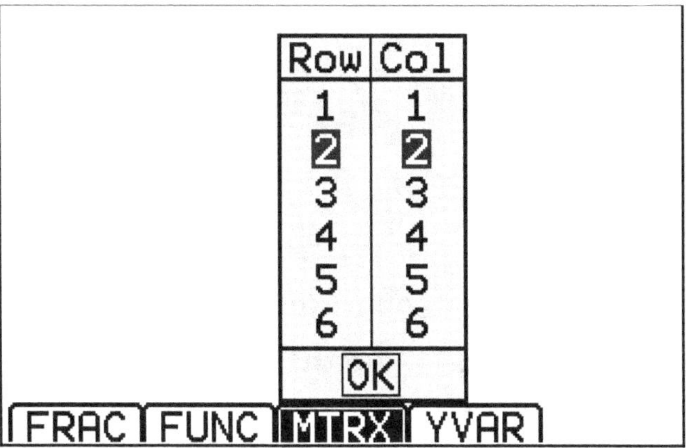

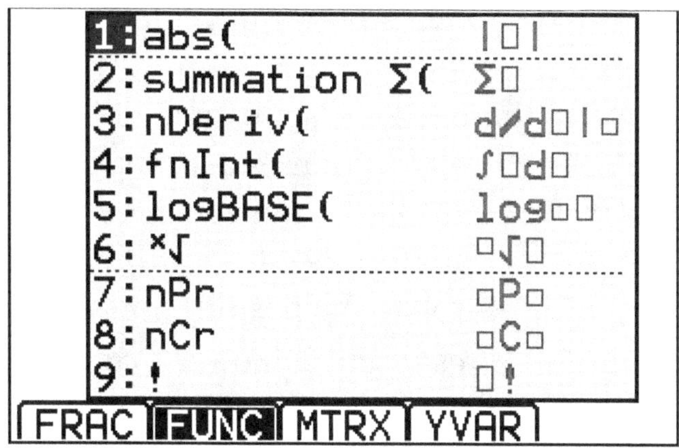

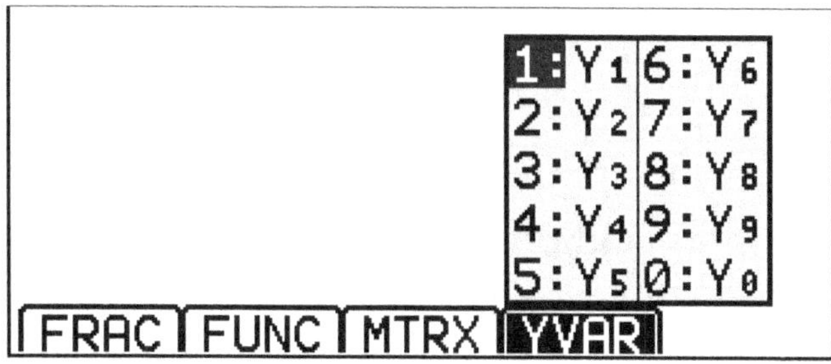

Once you're in the shortcut menu, you can also move from screen to screen with the cursor keys or by pressing one of the other graphing keys.

INSERTING OR DELETING

Uh-oh…you've put in $(-12)^2 + 5(-2)^2 + 13$ onto the home screen, but then you realize that that -2 should have been a -12 instead. You scroll back a bit to the 2, press 1, and yikes:

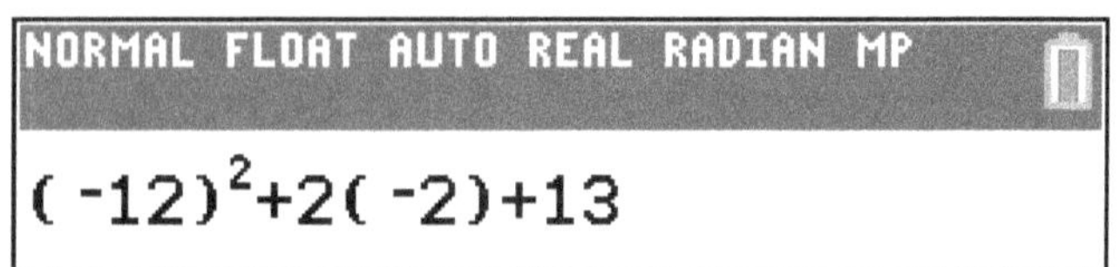

The calculator overwrites the 2 instead of putting the 1 in front. Stupid technology. Before you go relaxing and thinking that robots will not eventually be our masters, here is a way to insert a number instead of overwriting:

1. Scroll to the position you would like to insert the value.
2. Press 2nd del (2nd row, 3rd column). You'll notice that the black cursor now turns invisible.
3. Type in whatever you'd like in that position.

As long as you don't press the cursor keys, you can keep typing to insert values. Remember, the cursor is always on top of where you are about to add a value.

Similarly, there may be some times when you realize that you incorrectly typed a value that you need to delete. For example, suppose $(-12)^2 + 5(-2)^2 + 13$ should really have been $(-2)^2 + 5(-2)^2 + 13$, and you need to get rid of that pesky 1.

1. Scroll to the position you would like to delete the value.
2. Press del (2nd row, 3rd column).

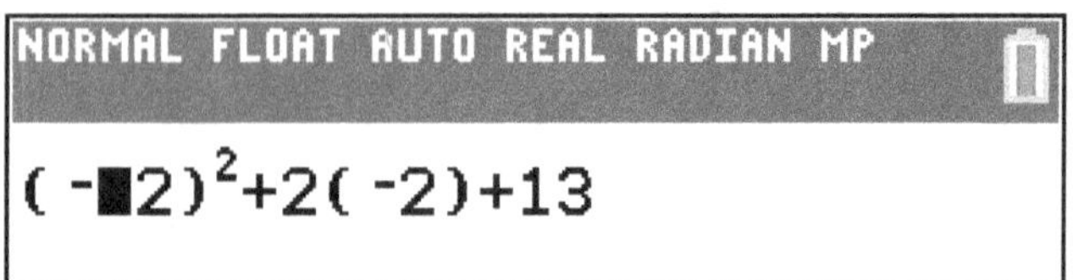

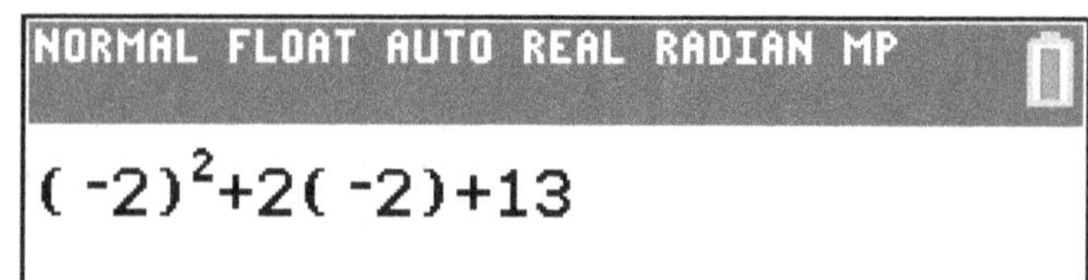

When you are in MATHPRINT mode, to get rid of exponents, you'll need to scroll to the exponent and press del twice—once to remove the actual exponent and the second time to remove the exponent template (the little box around where the exponent goes).

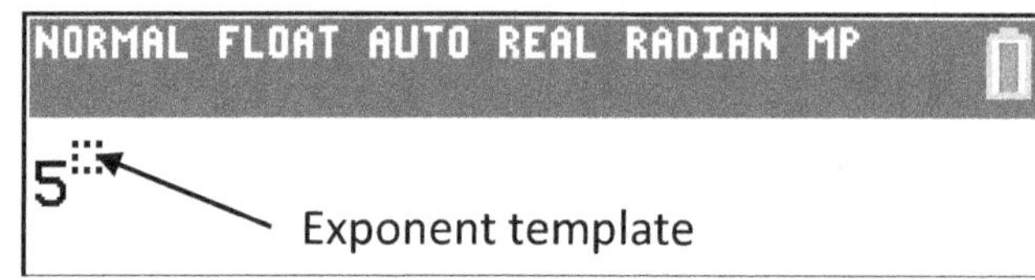

QUITTING

Some students never figure out how to quit back to the home screen and revert back to:

1. Turning the calculator on and off.
2. Taking out the batteries.

Come on! The smart people who made your calculator wouldn't forget to give you a way to go back from whence you came.

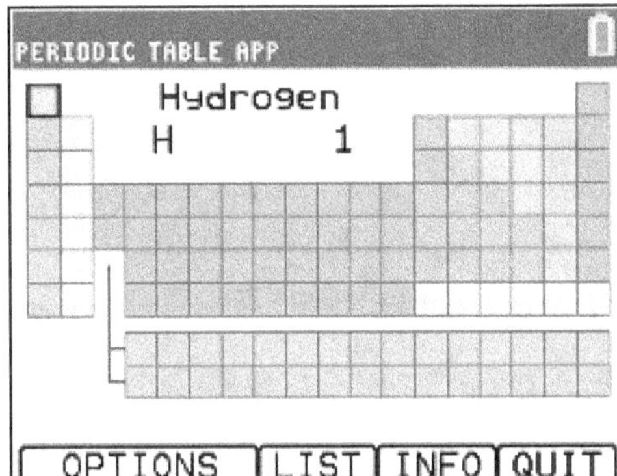

Uh-oh! I'm playing with the Periodic Table App (like all the cool kids), but I can't figure out how to get to that QUIT option on the bottom!

NOTE: You'd press the graph button to quit from that screen.

To quit a screen (return to home screen)

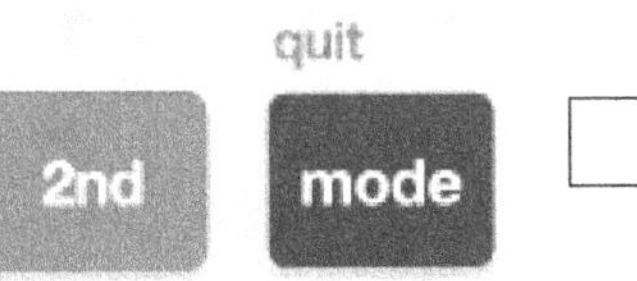

Help 'em out, Drizzy!

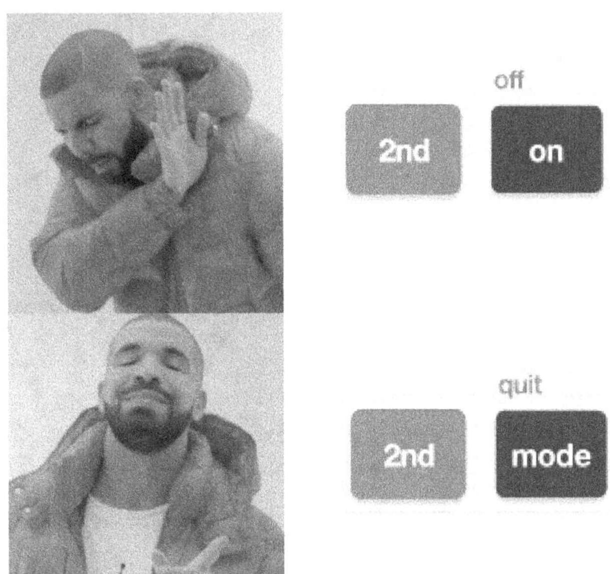

www.TestPrepWizards.com

STORING VALUES AND RECALLING STORED VALUES

Two of the most common mistakes students make on the calculator involve order of operations and parentheses usage. The storage button $\boxed{\text{sto} \rightarrow}$ (9th row, 1st column) can fix both of those issues in one fell swoop—especially when it is teamed up with the fraction option.

To store a value, press the following buttons:

A value represents any number. There are a few ways to bring up a variable.

1. Press the variable button $\boxed{x, T, \theta, n}$ (3rd row, 2nd column). This will store a variable as the default variable for your mode, which will almost certainly be x. **NOTE**: if pressing that button does not give you an x, press $\boxed{\text{mode}}$ and press $\boxed{\text{enter}}$ on the FUNCTION option that is a few lines down.
2. Press $\boxed{\text{alpha}}$ and any button that has a letter in green above.

EXAMPLE: Store 15 as x on the calculator.

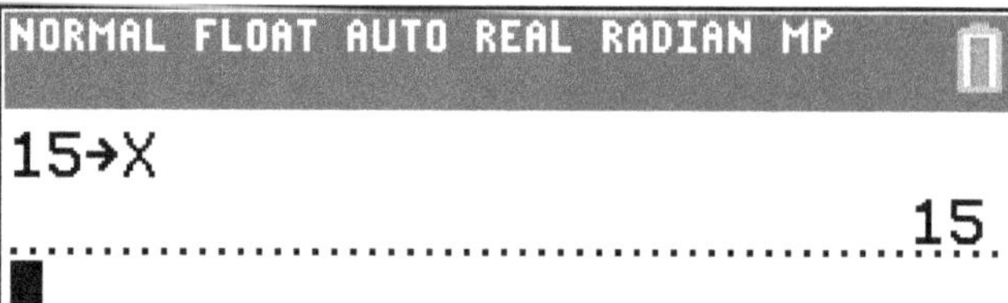

EXAMPLE: Store 0.5 as A on the calculator.

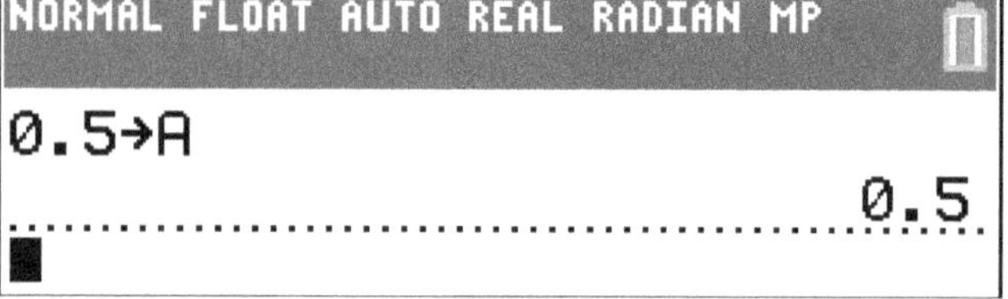

The benefit of using the $\boxed{\text{sto} \rightarrow}$ button is that now any time you put that variable on the home screen (until you overwrite the variable), the calculator thinks you want to used the stored value.

EXAMPLE: Evaluate $x^2 - 3x - 20$ when $x = 15$.

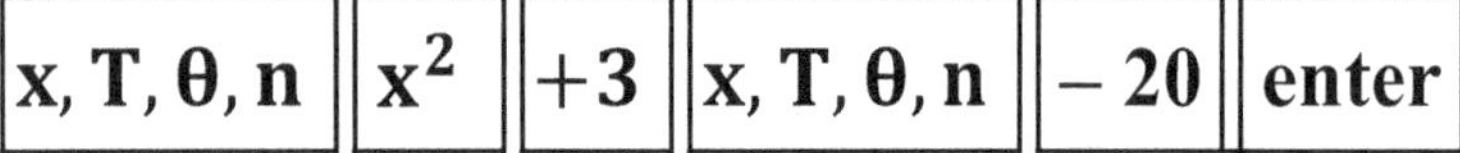

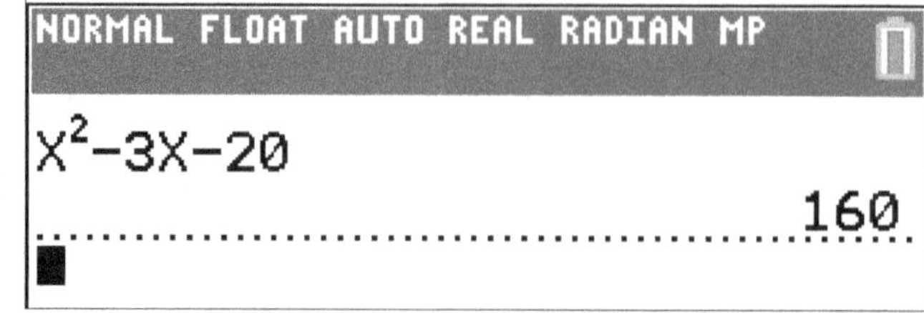

STORING VALUES AND RECALLING STORED VALUES

You can also solve questions that involve substituting in for multiple variables by storing values as different values and then recalling those variables.

EXAMPLE: What is the value of $x^2 + (y - 3)^2 + 2$ when $x = -5$ and $y = 2$?

1. Store x as -5: $\boxed{-5}$ $\boxed{\text{sto} \rightarrow}$ $\boxed{x, T, n, \theta}$
2. Store y as 2: $\boxed{2}$ $\boxed{\text{sto} \rightarrow}$ $\boxed{\text{alpha}}$ $\boxed{1}$
3. Write the expression on the home screen and press $\boxed{\text{enter}}$

```
-5→X
                                    -5
2→Y
                                     2
X²+(Y−3)²+2
                                    28
```

LIFE HACK: You can write all the expressions on one line if you separate the equations with the colon.

Colon (:) $\boxed{\textbf{alpha}}$ $\boxed{.}$

```
NORMAL FLOAT AUTO REAL RADIAN MP

-5→X:2→Y:X²+(Y−3)²+2
                                    28
```

Suppose you have a question like the following on the ACT:

48. What is the solution set of the equation
$x^4 + 5x^2 - 36 = 0$?

F. $\{-9, 4\}$

G. $\{-9, -2, 2\}$

H. $\{-3, 3, 4\}$

J. $\{-3, 3, -2i, 2i\}$

K. $\{-2, 2, -3i, 3i\}$

You know that you can work backwards with the answers, but you think it's inefficient to try to plug in *all* those answers. Let's see how to recall what's on the screen to make this a quickie.

STORING VALUES AND RECALLING STORED VALUES

Since each of the answer choices are potential answers, you can take advantage of the fact that any answer choice that doesn't satisfy the equation can automatically be eliminated.

48. What is the solution set of the equation
$x^4 + 5x^2 - 36 = 0$?

    F. $\{-9, 4\}$

    G. $\{-9, -2, 2\}$

    H. $\{-3, 3, 4\}$

    J. $\{-3, 3, -2i, 2i\}$

    K. $\{-2, 2, -3i, 3i\}$

STRATEGY: Store -9 as x and then input the equation $x^4 + 5x^2 - 36$ and press enter to see if the answer is 0.

NOTE: To raise x to the fourth power, press x, T, n, θ and then the caret $\boxed{\wedge}$ (5th row, 5th column). If you're in MATHPRINT, you should see a box to input the exponent. If you're in CLASSIC, you'll just see the caret after x.

Since you did not get 0 as the result, this means that -9 is not a possible solution. You can eliminate answer choices F and G.

```
-9→X
                        -9
X⁴+5X²-36
                      6930
```

Next, you'll probably want to check either -3 or 3 because they appear in two answer choices (if either did not give you 0, you'd eliminate H and J and have K as your answer).

To do this as simply as possible, overwrite what x means; that is, store -3 (or 3) as x. However, before retyping $x^4 + 5x^2 - 36$ and pressing enter to see if the answer is 0, use the arrow keys to scroll up to $x^4 + 5x^2 - 36$, and press enter twice. The first time you press enter, you'll repeat $x^4 + 5x^2 - 36$ on the home screen. The second time evaluates it with the new value of x. Since you do not get 0, the answer must be K.

```
HISTORY
-9→X
                        -9
X⁴+5X²-36
                      6930
-3→X
                        -3
```

```
NORMAL FLOAT AUTO REAL RADIAN MP
-9→X
                        -9
X⁴+5X²-36
                      6930
-3→X
                        -3
X⁴+5X²-36
                        90
```

STORING VALUES AND RECALLING STORED VALUES

NOTE: You can also scroll back through your history either by continually pressing the up arrow or with the entry option. The latter is accomplished by pressing $\boxed{\text{2nd}}$ $\boxed{\text{enter}}$ on any free line on your home screen.

There's a couple other ways to evaluate expressions on the calculator, most of which take advantage of the graphing button, $\boxed{\text{y} =}$.

The downside of these options is that you can only evaluate functions—that is, equations that look like $y =$ something with just x variables. However, it can be quicker when you need to evaluate a lot of values.

To begin, press the $\boxed{\text{y} =}$ button (1st row, 1st column). Many students are familiar with this button—it's what you'd use to graph a function. However, there are three ways to use it to calculate values. In our opinion, from least to most helpful, they are:

1. The **table** option
2. The **value** option
3. The **YVAR** option

To begin with, input a function into Y_1 (**NOTE:** you can input the function into any of the Y rows, but that will slightly change the next steps).

EXAMPLE: Input $x^3 - 3x^2 + 5x - 1$ into Y_1

```
NORMAL FLOAT AUTO REAL RADIAN MP

 Plot1   Plot2   Plot3
■\Y1■X^3-3X^2+5X-1■
```

To see a list of possible values, press $\boxed{\text{2nd}}$ $\boxed{\text{graph}}$.

You can scroll up or down (to see values less than 0 or greater than 10) on the table. The problem is that it's clunky to get values that are not integers. It can be done, but there are much easier ways to get values.

```
NORMAL FLOAT AUTO REAL RADIAN MP
PRESS + FOR ΔTbl
   X        Y1
   0        -1
   1        2
   2        5
   3        14
   4        35
   5        74
   6        137
   7        230
   8        359
   9        530
   10       749

X=0
```

STORING VALUES AND RECALLING STORED VALUES

The second way to get values is to press 2nd trace. This will bring up the **calc** menu.

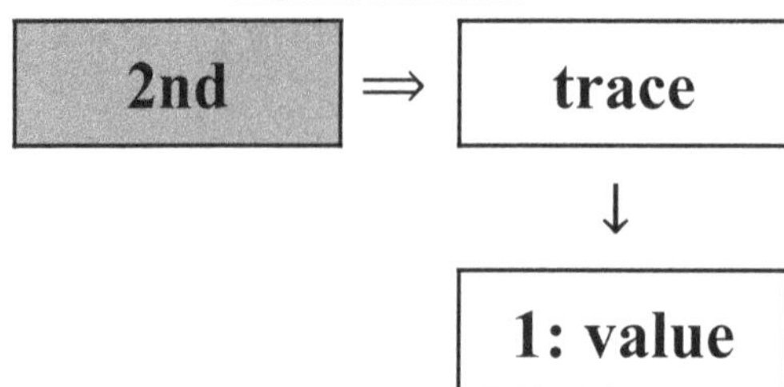

Either scrolling to **value** and pressing enter or pressing 1 will first graph the function and then ask you to input an x value in the lower left corner.

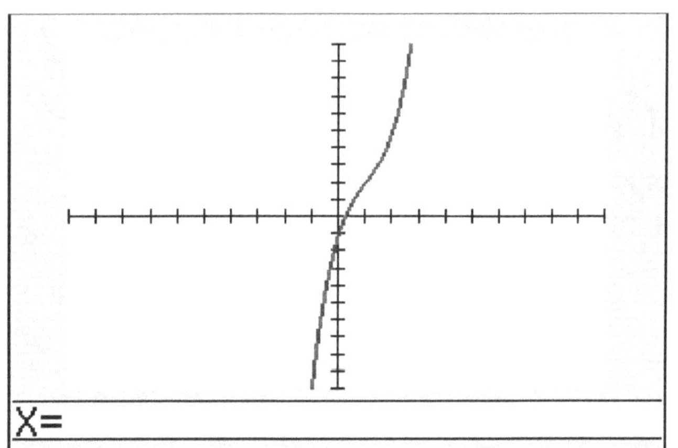

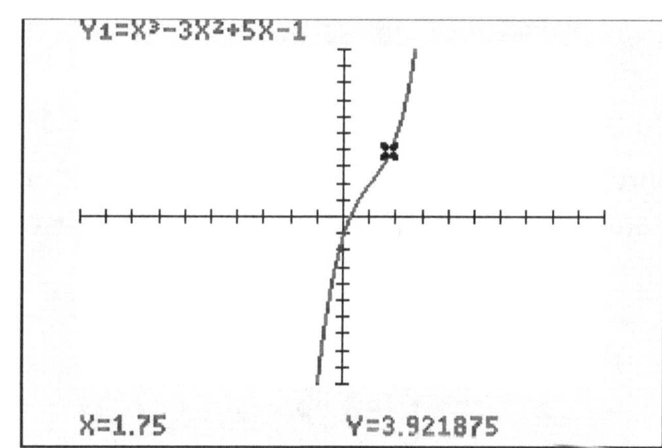

Just type in a value and press enter ; here, I am plugging in $x = 1.75$ to get $y = 3.921875$. **NOTE:** You can just type in another x value to overwrite the 1.75. You do not need to go back through 2nd trace to input more values.

Finally, what I think is the most efficient way: the **YVAR** option. There are two ways to bring this option up (I recommend the first approach):

Secret Menu		**vars Button**	
1.	alpha trace	1.	vars (4th row, 4th column)
2.	1 or enter	2.	Scroll right to **Y-VARS**
		3.	1 or enter
		4.	1 or enter

STORING VALUES AND RECALLING STORED VALUES

I'm going to use the secret menu option. You should get something that looks like this:

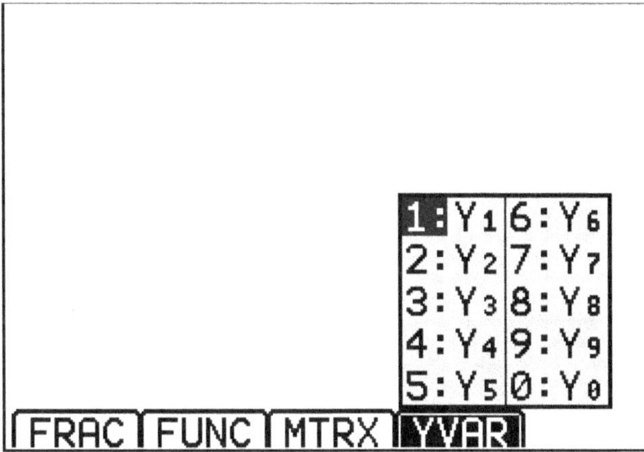

The **MOST IMPORTANT THING TO REMEMBER** is that you need to enclose the value you want to evaluate in parentheses. So, to calculate the value when $x = 1.75$, you should have:

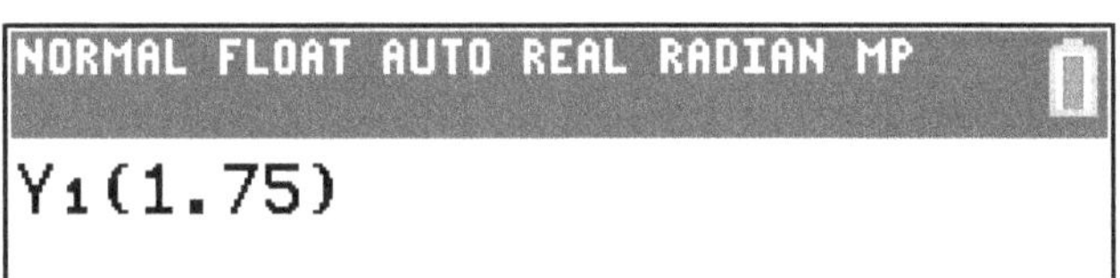
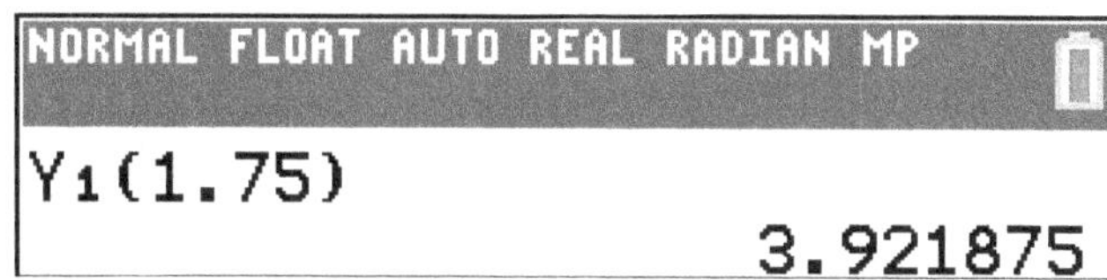

If you have more values to evaluate, you can just scroll back to $Y_1(1.75)$ and press enter to recall it. Next, just replace the 1.75 with whatever the new value you want to evaluate is.

It's usually a little quicker to use the **YVAR** option since you do not need to wait for the graph to initially get graphed.

You can also solve composite functions using the **YVARS** option.

48. The functions f and g are defined as $f(x) = 2x + 3$ and $g(x) = 5x - 1$. What is the value of $f(g(-2))$?

    F. -19

    G. -11

    H. -1

    J. 1

    K. 11

STORING VALUES AND RECALLING STORED VALUES

A composition of functions means you substitute one function into another—much easier when you have actual values. To solve:

1. Put the first function, $f(x)$, into Y_1 by pressing $\boxed{y=}$ and then $\boxed{2}\ \boxed{x, T, n, \theta}\ \boxed{+3}$

2. Put the second function, g(x), into Y_2 by pressing $\boxed{y=}$ and then $\boxed{5}\ \boxed{x, T, n, \theta}\ \boxed{-3}$.

3. Quit back to the home screen by pressing $\boxed{2nd}\ \boxed{mode}$.

4. Use the shortcut menu for **YVAR** to enter Y_1 and open a set of parentheses. Your screen should look like this:

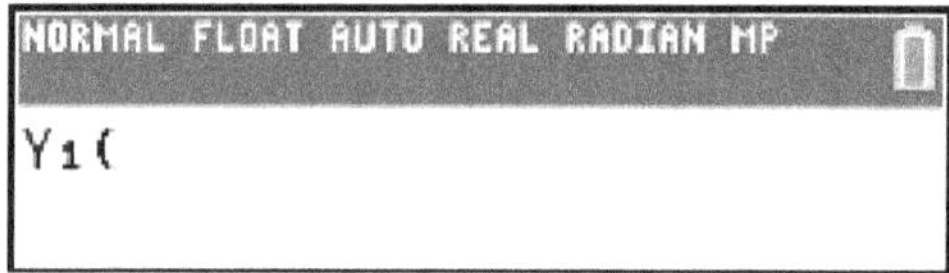

5. Use the shortcut menu for **YVAR** to enter Y_2 and put -2 in parentheses. You screen should now look like this:

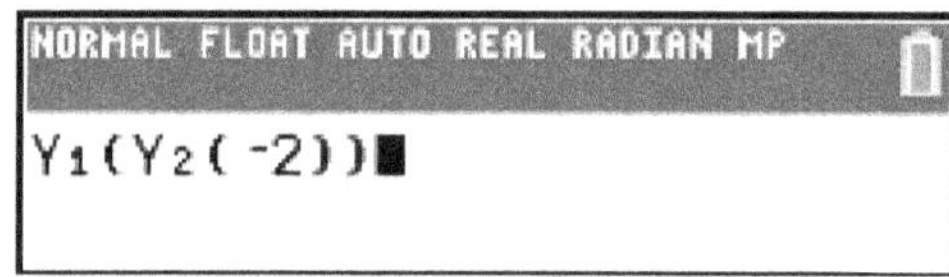

6. Finally, put a closing parentheses (for the Y_1) and press $\boxed{enter}$. Voila!

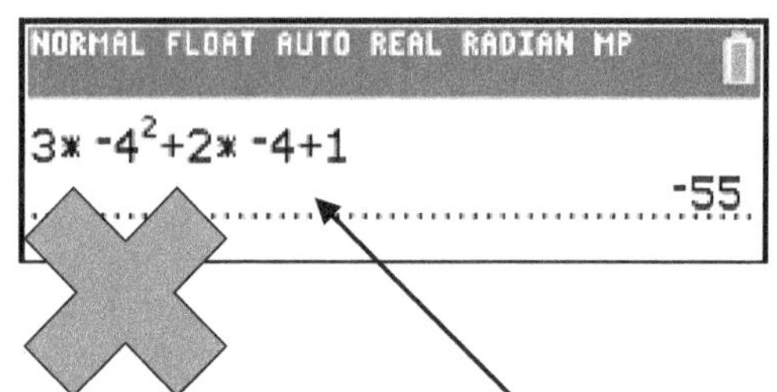

One final word on the power of storing numbers—who hasn't been here?

EXAMPLE: What is the value of $3x^2 + 2x + 1$ if $x = -4$?

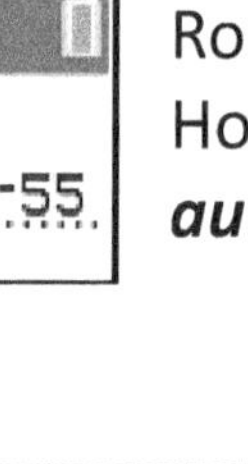

Rookie mistake! That -4 needs to be in parentheses. However, notice that if I store -4 as X, then the calculator *automatically applies the order of operations*.

This may seem correct, but for the first term, your calculator thinks you want to square the 4, multiply by -1 (the negative), then multiply by 3.

FOCUSED EXAMPLES

EXAMPLES TO TRY ON YOUR CALCULATOR

		Answer
1.	What is the value of $5x^2 - 11$ if $x = -4$?	**69**
2.	What is the value of $a^3 + 5a - \sqrt{a}$ if $a = 9$?	**771**
3.	What is the value of $x^x + 5^x$ if $x = 3$?	**152**
4.	What is the value of $a^2b + b^2a$ if $a = 5$ and $b = -2$?	**−30**
5.	If $f(x) = \sqrt{2x - 3} + 5$, what is the value of $f(14)$?	**10**
6.	If $f(x) = x^3 + 1$ and $g(x) = 1 - 2x$, what's the value of $f(g(-2))$?	**126**
7.	If $f(x) = x^3 + 1$ and $g(x) = 1 - 2x$, what's the value of $g(f(-2))$?	**15**
8.	If $f(x) = \dfrac{x^2 + 3x + 7}{x + 2}$, what is the value of $f(3)$?	**5**
9.	If $f(x) = \dfrac{x^2 + 1}{x + 2}$ and $g(x) = 3 - x^2$, what is the value of $f(g(-1))$?	**5/4 or 1.25**
10.	If $f(x) = \dfrac{x^2 + 1}{x + 2}$ and $g(x) = 3 - x^2$, what is the value of $g(f(-1))$?	**−1**

SOLVING EQUATIONS

Since the calculator allows you to substitute in values and solve, it's only natural to ask, "Does the calculator solve for a variable?" The answer? Sort of. Here are two ways that you can kind of solve for a variable.

There are two ways to solve equations:

1. The Equation Solver
2. The app PLYSMLT2

Since not all apps come preloaded on the calculator, I'll discuss PLYSMLT2 in the APPtly named APPendix (har har har).

To bring up the equation solver, select:

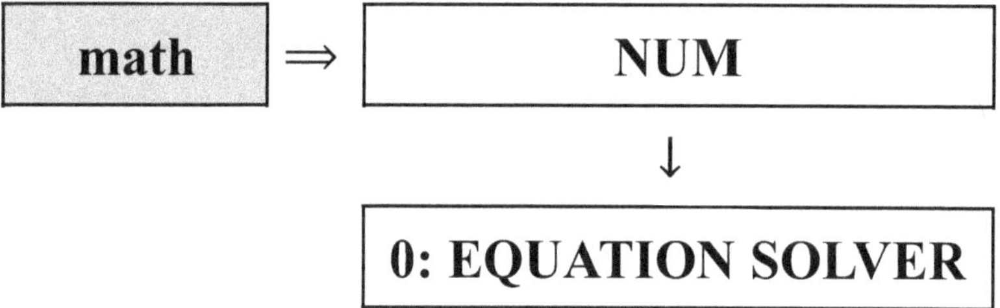

| **math** | $\Rightarrow$ | **NUM** |

$\downarrow$

0: EQUATION SOLVER

NOTE: On certain versions, "Equation Solver" may be replaced with:

C: NUMERIC SOLVER

Regardless of what your calculator calls it, you'll see a screen that looks like this:

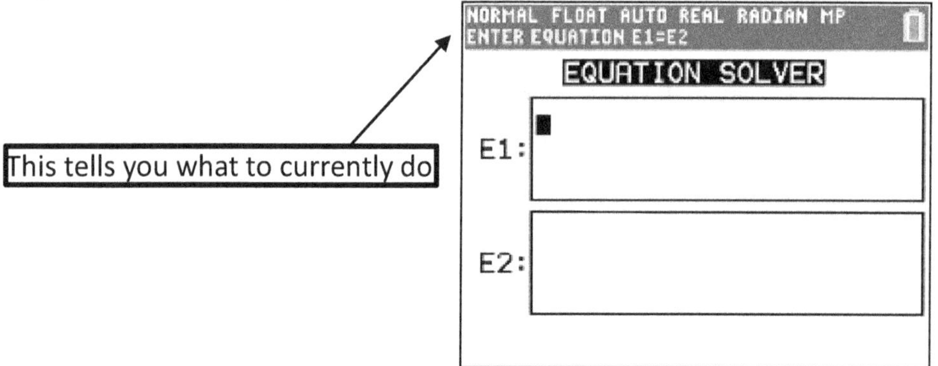

The top of the screen says E1=E2, so we need two equations; many times, the second equation will simply be a number.

SOLVING EQUATIONS

Suppose we had the following question:

26. What value of x solves the following equation?

$$\frac{x^2 + 5x + 6}{x + 3} = 4$$

    F. -3

    G. -1

    H. 1

    J. 2

    K. 3

Now, we could solve this by working backwards with the answer choices and using the `sto →` button or the **YVARS** option. In this example, though, we're going to use **EQUATION SOLVER (NUMERIC SOLVER).**

First off, let's talk about how to write fractions—and I don't mean with the `÷` button and a bunch of parentheses! Despite all the amazing things these calculators do, many of our students are floored by the fact that the calculator *can actually write fractions* on the home screen.

There are two ways to access the fraction menu:

1.   The secret menu `alpha` `y =` .

2.   Through the `math` and then scrolling right to FRAC.

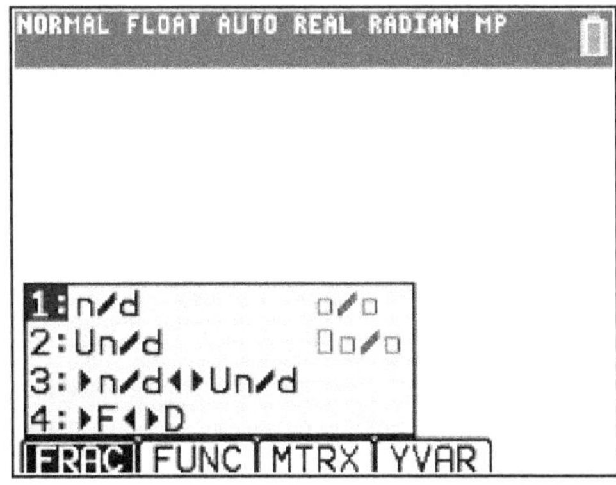

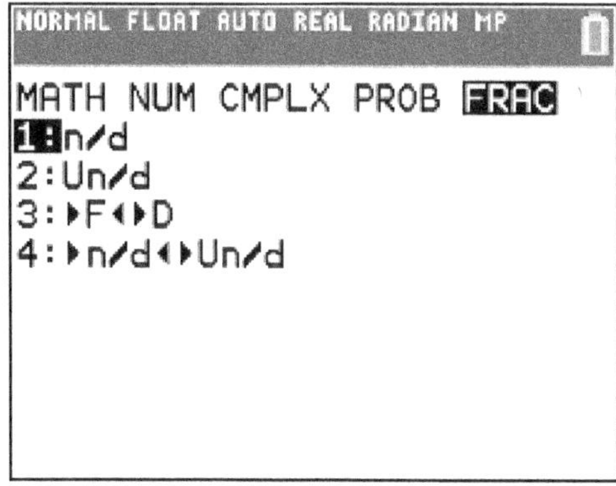

SOLVING EQUATIONS

The four options you have (we'll be using each in a few pages):

1. **n/d:** Writes a fraction template on your home screen (the n stands for numerator, and the d stands for denominator).
2. **Un/d**: Writes a mixed number template on your home screen (the U stands for unit, and the n and d are numerator and denominator, respectively).
3. **▶n/d ◀▶Un/d**: Takes an fraction and, if possible, rewrites it as a mixed number. Only works if your fraction is **improper** (that is, the numerator is greater than the denominator).
4. **▶F ◀▶D:** Takes a fraction (F) and turns it into a decimal (D). Helpful when you have a fraction written on your screen and do not want to use the $\boxed{\div}$.

Since $\frac{x^2+5x+6}{x+3} = 4$, we want to take advantage of the **n/d** option to input the rational function on the left side of the equation.

In our equation, we have $E1 = \frac{x^2+5x+6}{x+3}$ and $E2 = 4$. Let's put that into our **NUMERIC SOLVER**:

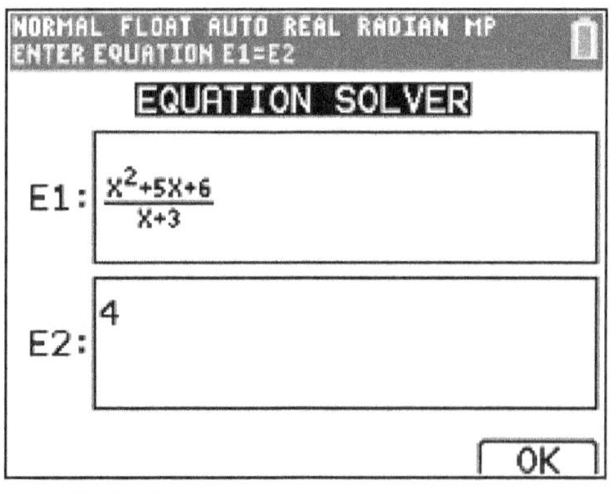

This moves us from E1's field to E2's field

SOLVING EQUATIONS

Once we've gotten everything input, there are two ways to progress forward:

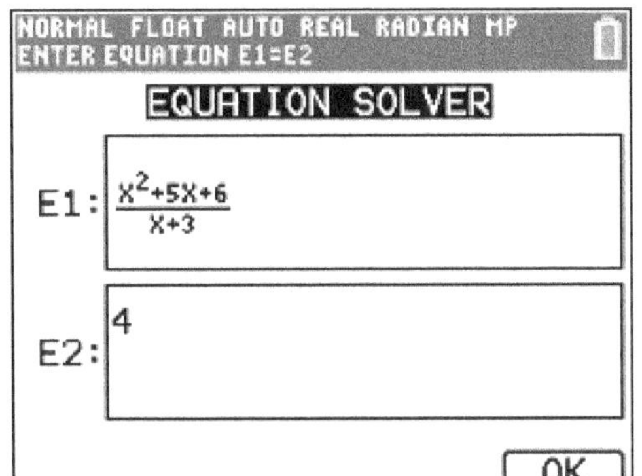

1. Use the down arrow to scroll to the next screen.

2. Press the graph button to proceed to the next screen.

Your next screen should look like this (**NOTE:** you probably don't have an $X = 11$ and that's fine):

Here's where many students make mistakes.

YOUR ANSWER IS NOT THE X VALUE YOU CURRENTLY SEE!

At this screen, your calculator is waiting for you to guess what the answer is. At the top of the screen, it's changed what it says.

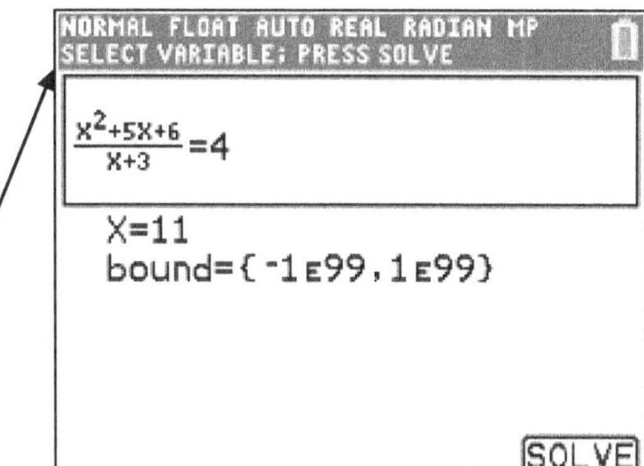

Let's explain the two new options:

1. The $X = \#$: This is your guess for an answer. For "simple" equations, it doesn't really need to be close to the actual answer. However, when you have multiple solutions, you may not get the desired solution if your guess is closer to another solution.
2. bound $= \{-1E99, 1E99\}$: This is the interval you are looking for a solution in (the **domain** you are searching). The value of X *must* be in this interval. $-1E99$ is basically $-\infty$ and $1E99$ is basically ∞. If you don't have a reason to change the bound, leave it as is.

To find the <u>actual</u> solution, you'll want to put a number in the $X =$ option, change the bounds (by scrolling down) if necessary, and then hit SOLVE. To solve, you use the graph button.

SOLVING EQUATIONS

Voila! Once you hit the SOLVE button, you should see something like this:

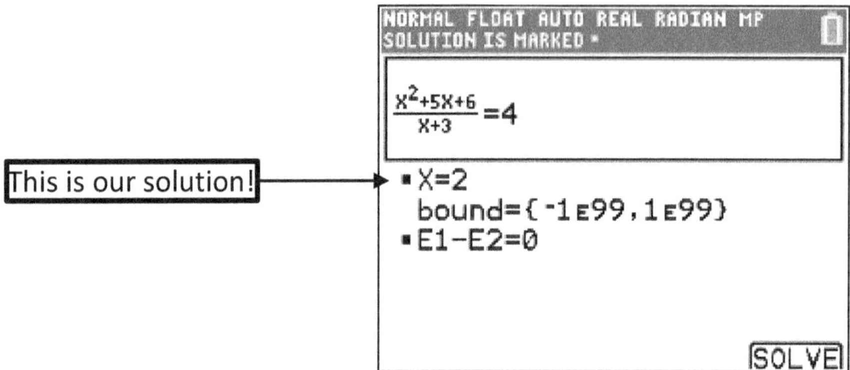

Sometimes, you do need to actually worry about the bounds—especially if you are working with **quadratics** (equations in which the highest power is 2 and other exponents are nonnegative whole numbers). Consider homeboy right here:

34. What values of x are solutions to $2x^2 + 5x - 12 = 0$?

    F. $x = -4$ and $x = 1.5$

    G. $x = -4$ and $x = 3$

    H. $x = -3$ and $x = 4$

    J. $x = -1.5$ and $x = 4$

    K. $x = 1.5$ and $x = 4$

The answer choices are going to help us with the bounds. Since one value is negative and one value is positive in answers **F, G, H,** and **J**, we can first break the bounds up as all negative numbers,

$$\text{bound} = \{-1E99, 0\}$$

and then use process of elimination.

Note: If we do not return a solution, the answer must be **K** (why?).

Once you move to the guess screen, make sure you guess a negative number. In our example, I used $X = -1$ as a guess.

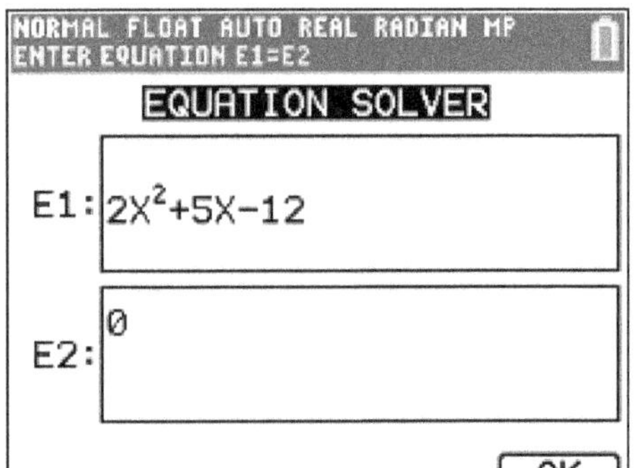

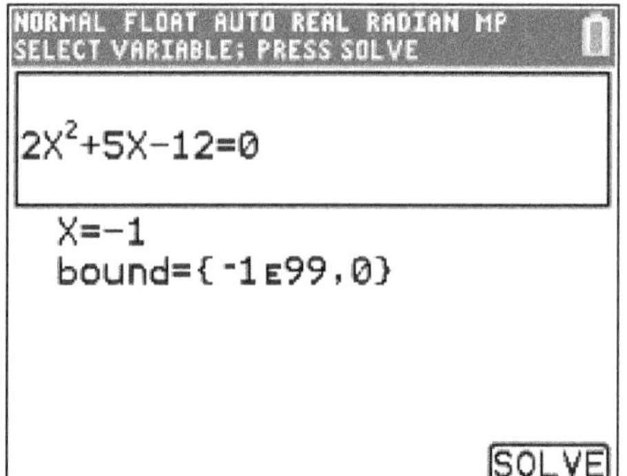

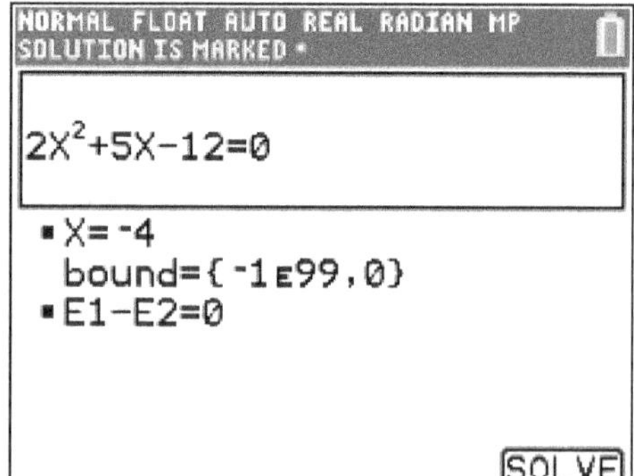

From here, we can eliminate answers **H, J,** and **K**, since none of those have $x = -4$ as a solution. All that is left is to run it back with positive bounds and a positive guess.

SOLVING EQUATIONS

Notice that setting an upper bound of 100 is good enough (in fact, anything larger than 3 would've been sufficient). Because of how the calculator is arriving at the answer, you may not get an exact answer like I did, but it will be close enough to know the answer is **F.**

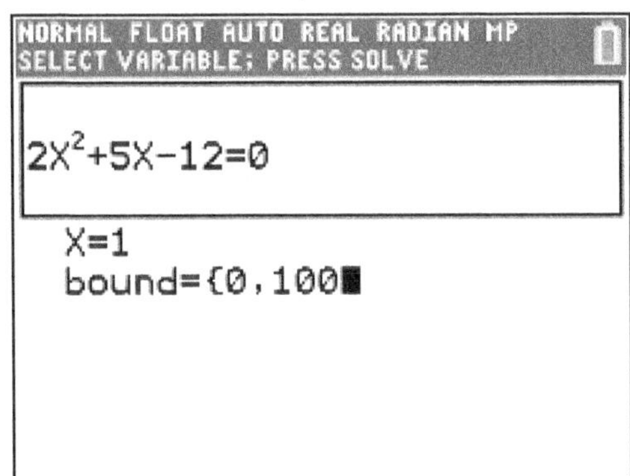

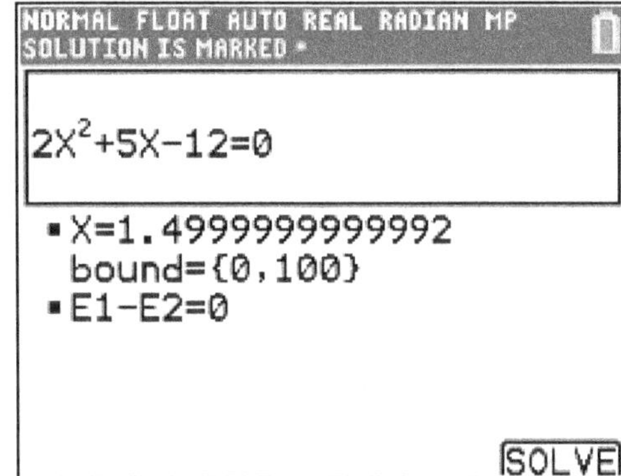

See, if you change the bounds or the guesses, you can end up with a different value. Regardless, you should be close enough to get the answer from the choices on the ACT.

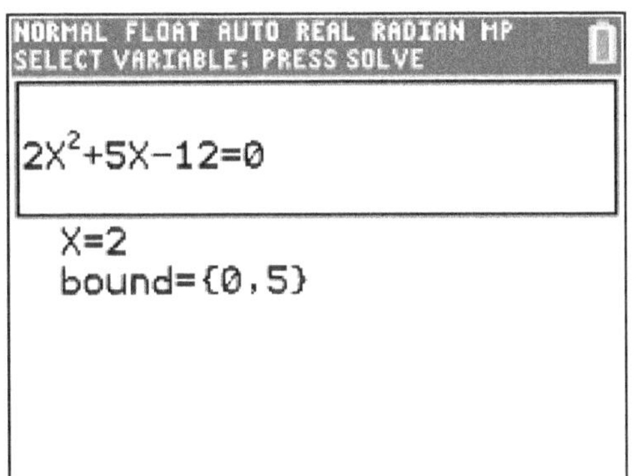

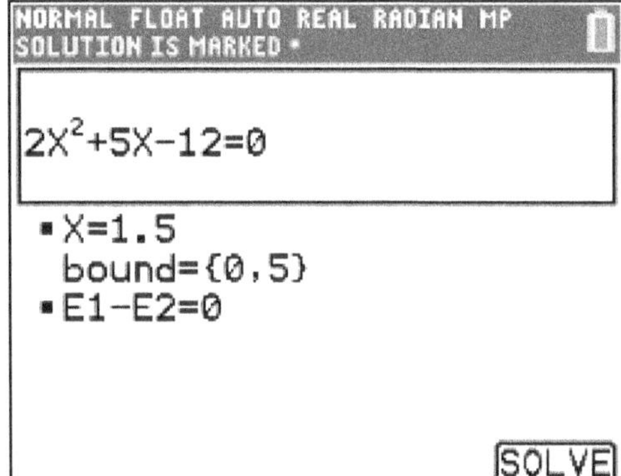

To quit out of the numeric solver, hit **2ⁿᵈ** **mode** .

FOCUSED EXAMPLES

EXAMPLES TO TRY ON YOUR CALCULATOR

		Answer
1.	Find the value of x if $3x + 8 = 35$	9
2.	Find the value of x if $5 - 2x = 13$	-4
3.	Find the value of x if $2x + 3 = 5x - 18$	7
4.	Find the value of x if $7x - 11 = 3x + 2$	$\frac{13}{4}$ or 3.25
5.	Find the value of x if $x^2 + 9x - 70 = 0$	5 and -14
6.	Find the value of x if $3x^2 + 13x = 10$	5 and $-\frac{2}{3}$
7.	Find the value of x if $3^x = 729$	6
8.	Find the value of x if $x^3 + x^2 - 9x - 9 = 0$	$-3, -1,$ and 3
9.	Find the value of x if $2^{-x} + x = 1$	-1 and 0
10.	Find the value of x if $5(x + 2)^2 - 3x = 26$	-3.722 and 0.322

FRACTIONS

My grandpappy had a saying about parentheses: "It's better to have 'em and not need 'em than to need 'em and not have 'em."

I know, I had weird life lessons in my family. We've all probably dealt with the annoyance of trying to put in the correct number of parentheses, only to end up with a wrong answer.

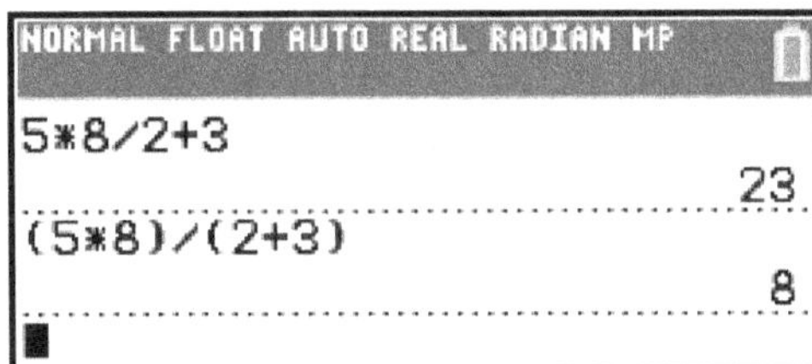

All the calculator knows is PEMDAS. In the top example, the calculator first multiplies 5 and 8 to get 40. Next, it divides that result by 2 to get 20. Finally, it adds 3 to arrive at 23.

In the bottom example, the calculator divides 40 by 5.

Well, I never had the heart to tell grandpappy that parentheses are mostly useless when you use the fraction option on the calculator.

1. Using the **fraction** option in the math:

2. Using the secret menu:

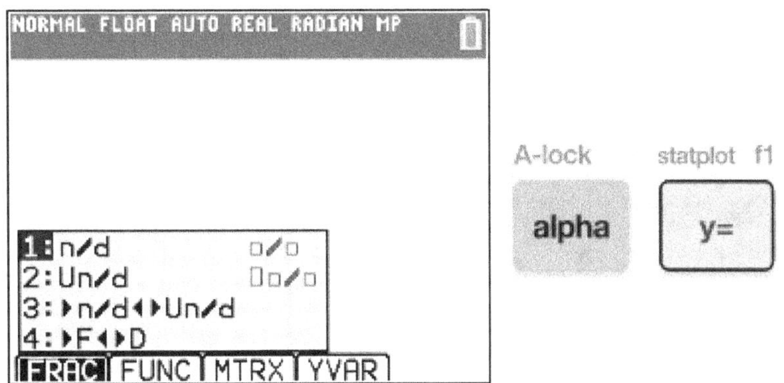

I generally use the second way because it's less keystrokes. #TimeManagement

FRACTIONS

Since I anticipate that you're not printing this eBook out, I can repeat information. If you've been progressing through this book in order, you've seen this in the solving equations section.

1. **n/d:** Writes a fraction template on your home screen (the n stands for numerator and the d stands for denominator).

2. **Un/d**: Writes a mixed number template on your home screen (the U stands for unit, and the n and d are numerator and denominator, respectively.)

3. **▶n/d ◀▶Un/d**: Takes an fraction and, if possible, rewrites it as a mixed number. Only works if your fraction is **improper:** that is, the numerator is greater than the denominator.

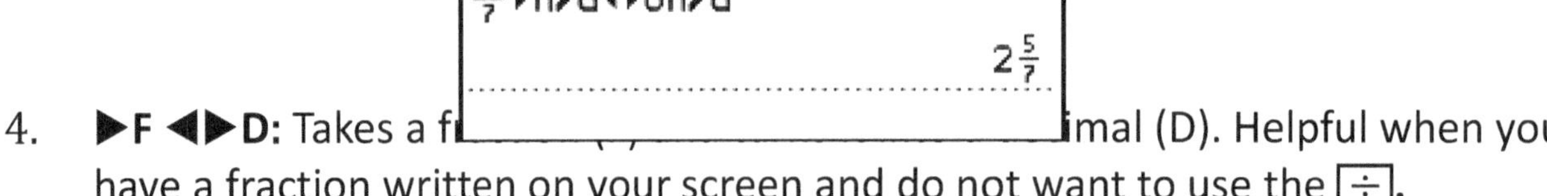

4. **▶F ◀▶D:** Takes a fraction (F) and rewrites it as a decimal (D). Helpful when you have a fraction written on your screen and do not want to use the ÷ .

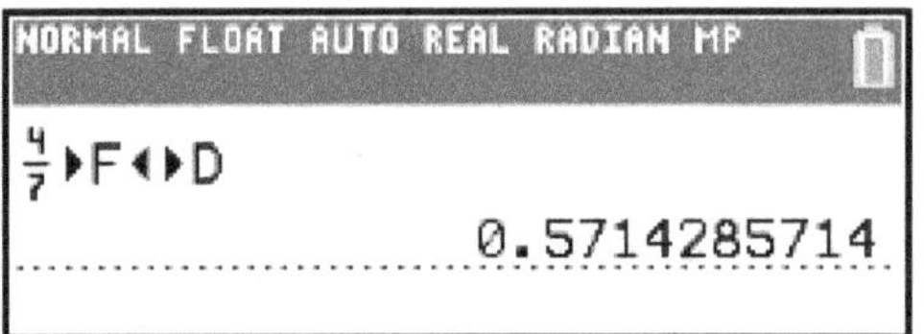

FRACTIONS

Why waste time converting to decimals or playing with parentheses on the ACT?

32. $\dfrac{3}{5} - \dfrac{2}{3}\left(\dfrac{1}{6} + \dfrac{2}{3}\right) = ?$

    F. $-\dfrac{1}{12}$

    G. $-\dfrac{1}{10}$

    H. $\dfrac{2}{45}$

    J. $\dfrac{1}{6}$

    K. $\dfrac{52}{45}$

By using the **fraction** template, you can ensure that what you are about to find is correct because your home screen will look exactly like what is on the page.

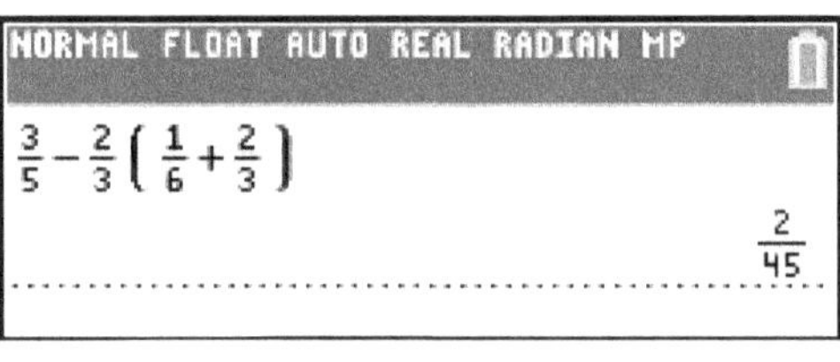

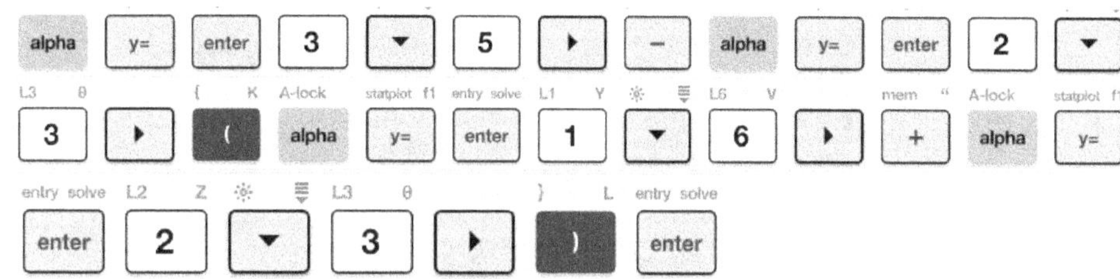

Don't be intimidated by number of keystrokes. It's basically just putting in a fraction a bunch of times. I timed myself—it took around 5 seconds to put that into the calculator.

What about a *nested fraction*? That is, a fraction that is part of another fraction. How meta.

16. $\dfrac{2 + \dfrac{1}{3}}{3 + \dfrac{1}{6}} = ?$

    F. $\dfrac{14}{19}$

    G. $\dfrac{7}{3}$

    H. $\dfrac{41}{18}$

    J. $\dfrac{8}{3}$

    K. $\dfrac{133}{18}$

All you need to do is input a fraction in the numerator of your fraction template and then repeat for the denominator.

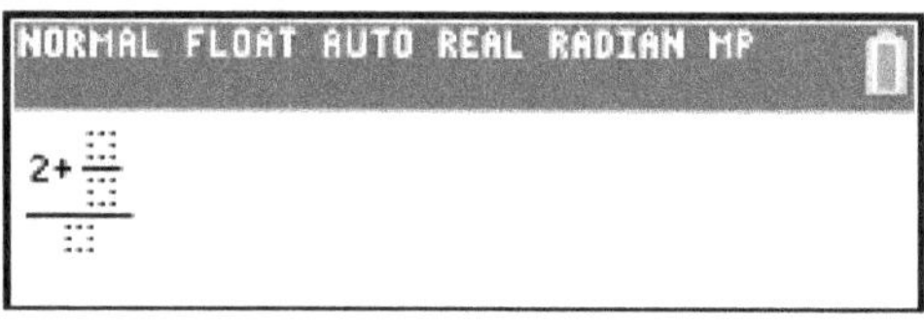

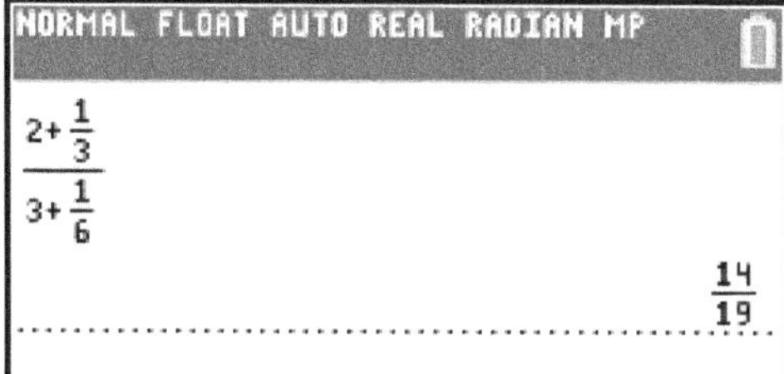

www.TestPrepWizards.com

ABSOLUTE VALUE

For many students, absolute value is a topic that is so far back in their math histories that they make preventable mistakes on what should be easier questions. There are two ways to work with absolute values on your calculator:

1. Using the **abs(** option in the math.

2. Using the secret menu.

You already know how I feel about the secret menu. Either way you access absolute value, you'll end up with a screen that looks like the following.

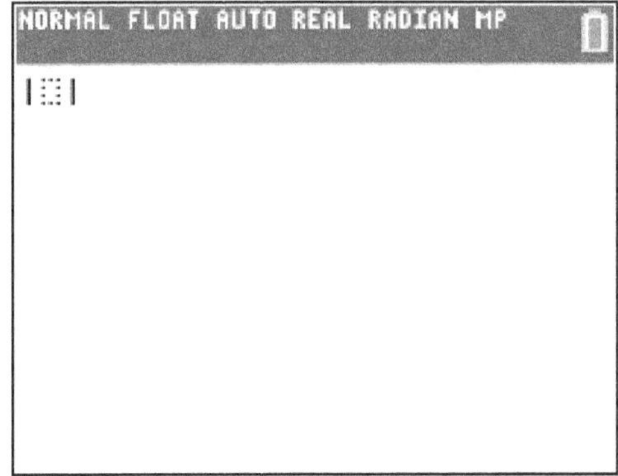

www.TestPrepWizards.com

ABSOLUTE VALUE

Once again, the calculator will perform all the necessary order of operations for you.

10. $|8 - 3| - |-6 - 2|$

    F. -3

    G. 1

    H. 7

    J. 13

    K. 19

A common mistake is to "distribute" the absolute value signs and make everything positive:

$$|8| + |3| + |-6| + |2|$$

Using the **abs(** option on the calculator prevents mistakes.

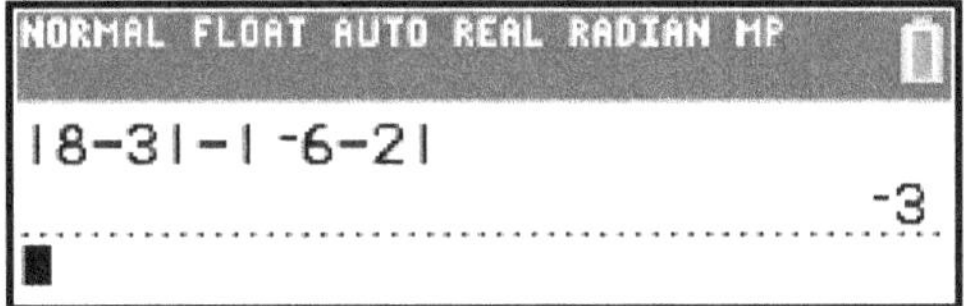

You combine concepts to calculate multiple operations at once.

18. What is the value of the expression
$$\frac{|-4-3|^2+(-3)^2}{20\div4\times3-1} \; ?$$

    F. $\dfrac{5}{7}$

    G. $\dfrac{20}{7}$

    H. $\dfrac{58}{11}$

    J. 15

    K. 60

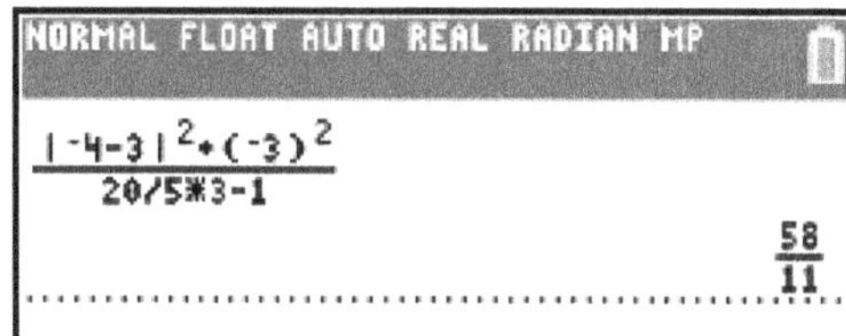

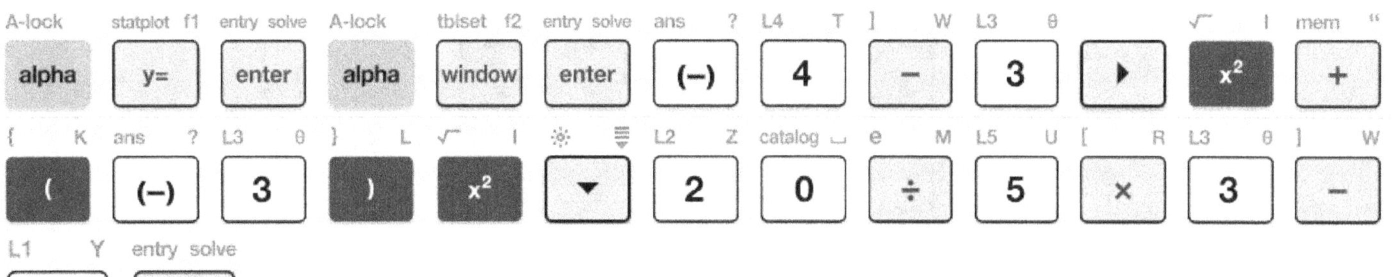

www.TestPrepWizards.com

ROOTS

Although many questions involving roots revolve around simplifying an exponent under a root (e.g. $\sqrt[5]{x^{20}}$), if you have a coefficient that also needs to be rooted, you can use the calculator to evaluate it.

1. Using the $\sqrt[x]{}$ option in the $\boxed{\text{math}}$

2. Using the secret menu.

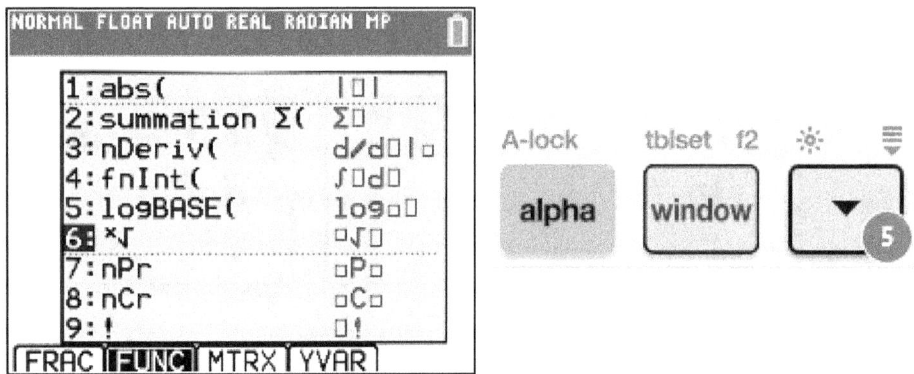

No matter how you get there, the result will be the same:

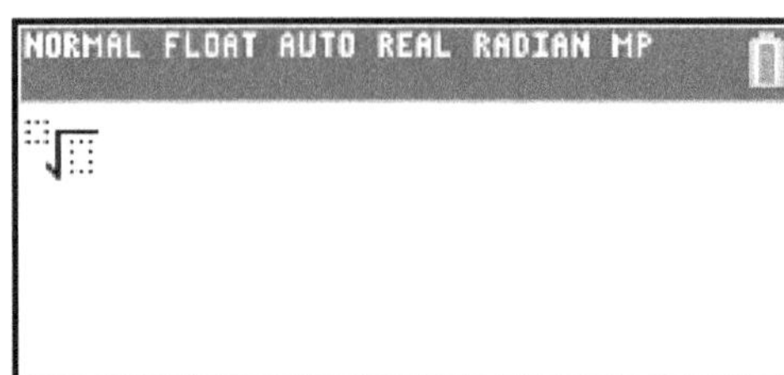

NOTE: on some calculator versions, you may have to put in the root first (5 for a fifth root) and then go through the steps above. Try it now to see what you need to do. Don't wait until test day to try it out

ROOTS

You may notice in the math menu that you have a **cube root** option:

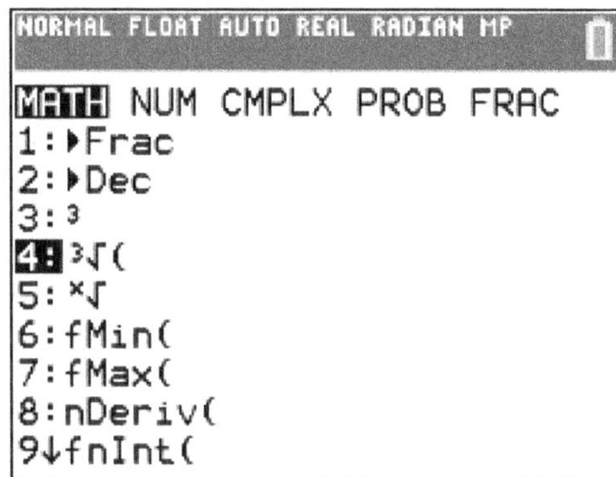

Also, although you can take a square root this way…

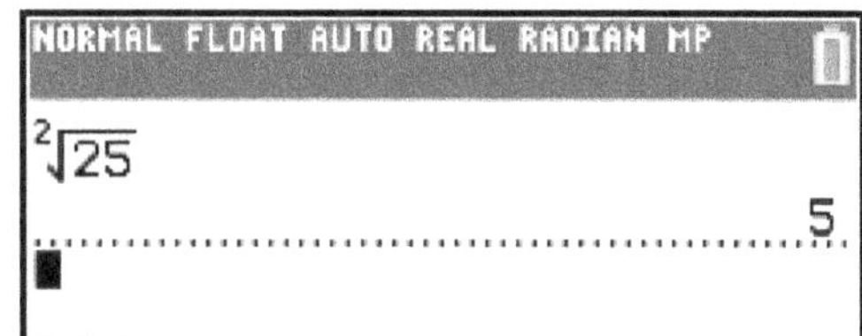

…that's kinda weird and your friends will judge you for it. Just use the **square root** function:

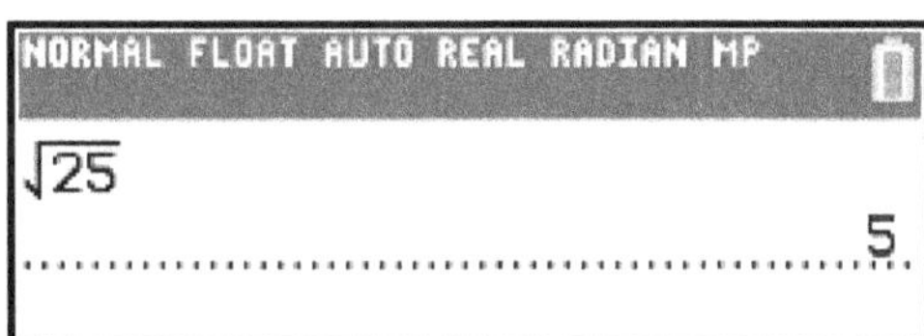

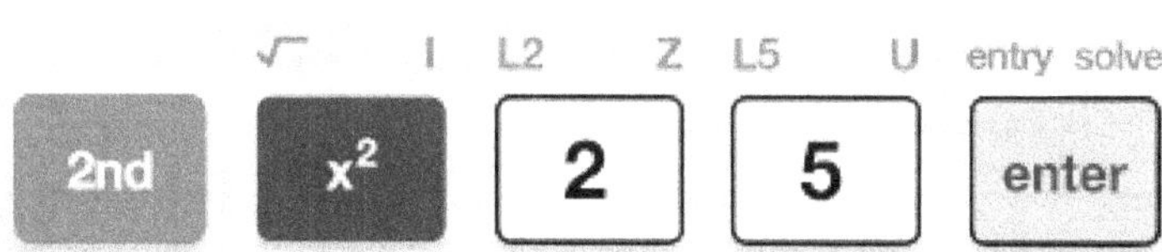

34. Which of the following is equivalent to $\sqrt[4]{256x^8y^{12}}$?

   F. $4x^2y^3$

   G. $4x^4y^8$

   H. $64x^2y^3$

   J. $64x^4y^8$

   K. $256x^2y^3$

Even if you don't know how to handle the part with variables, if you realize that you can take the fourth root of 256, you can get the answer down to **F** or **G**.

ROOTS

Again, you can combine multiple concepts to crush the ACT into submission.

42. Which of the following is equivalent to $\frac{2+\sqrt{3}}{5-\sqrt{3}}$?

F. $-\frac{3}{5}$

G. $\frac{1+2\sqrt{3}}{22}$

H. $\frac{7}{5}$

J. $\frac{13+7\sqrt{3}}{22}$

K. $\frac{13+7\sqrt{3}}{16}$

The calculator does not rationalize denominators (you can accomplish that with programs through—check out our website!).

However, we can still arrive at the correct answer with the calculator.

First, approximate the value of $\frac{2+\sqrt{3}}{5-\sqrt{3}}$ on the calculator:

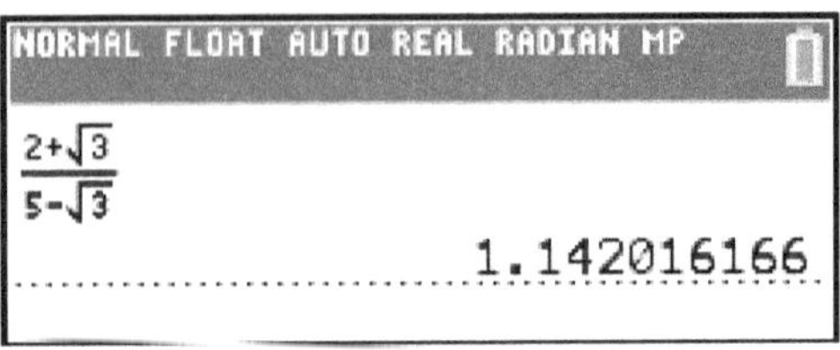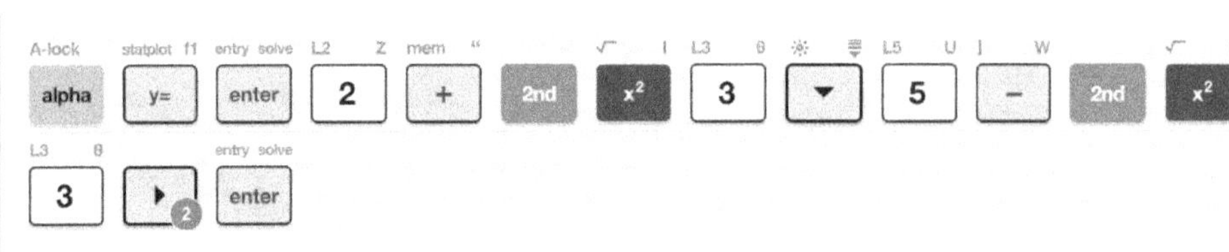

This automatically rules out **F** since it's negative. If you know that $\frac{7}{5} = 1.4$, then **H** is out as well. If not, just divide 7 by 5 on the calculator. Next, plug the answer choices into your calculator to see which one is the winner.

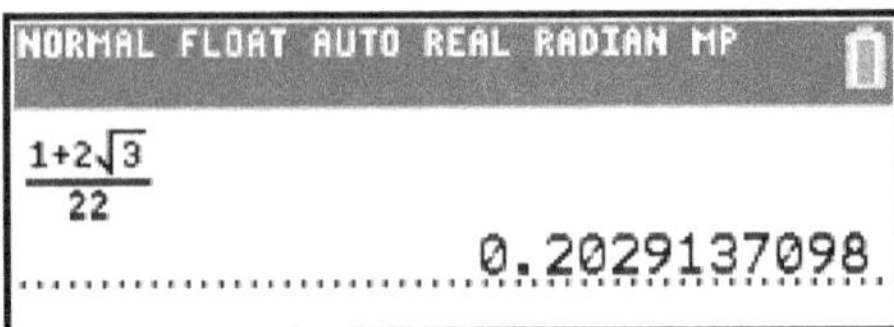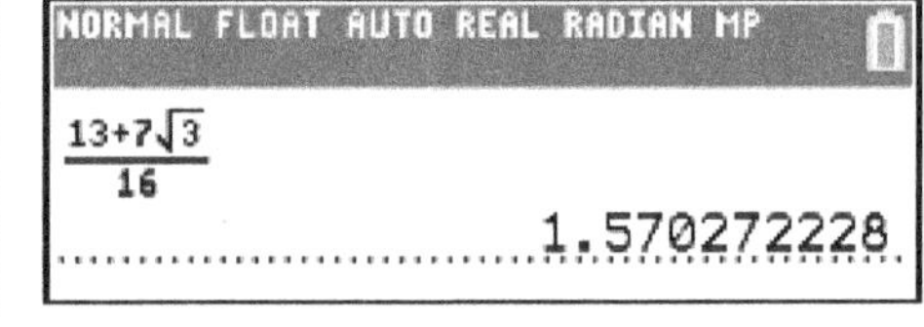

Not **G**	**J** lookin' tasty.	Not **K**

Remember, the ACT only cares whether you bubble in the correct answer, not how you got there. Recognizing which questions can be done on the calculator instead of the "school way" can not only get you a few more questions correct but also potentially save you time.

Even if you remember to multiply the numerator and denominator by the conjugate of the denominator, you can still check your work to ensure you haven't made a preventable mistake that the test writers anticipated.

COMPLEX NUMBERS

Even if you do not know that $i = \sqrt{-1}$, you can still get many questions involving **imaginary numbers** correct on the ACT through recognition.

1.   Finding i:

Once you know where i lives, you can simply plop it onto the home screen whenever you see it in a question.

44. For $i = \sqrt{-1}$, $(2 + 3i)^2 = ?$

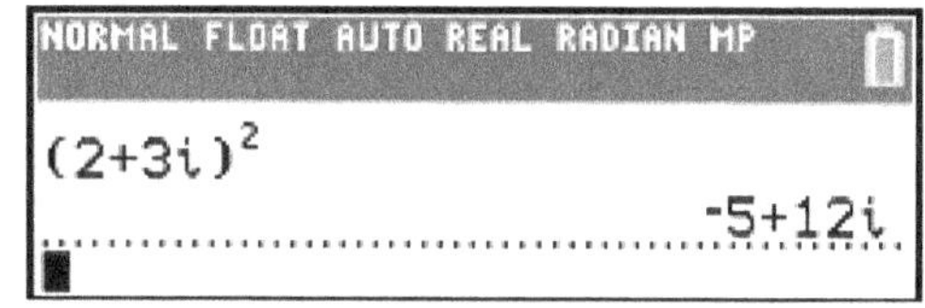

F. $-5 + 12i$

G. $1 + 12i$

H. $4 + 6i$

J. -5

K. -9

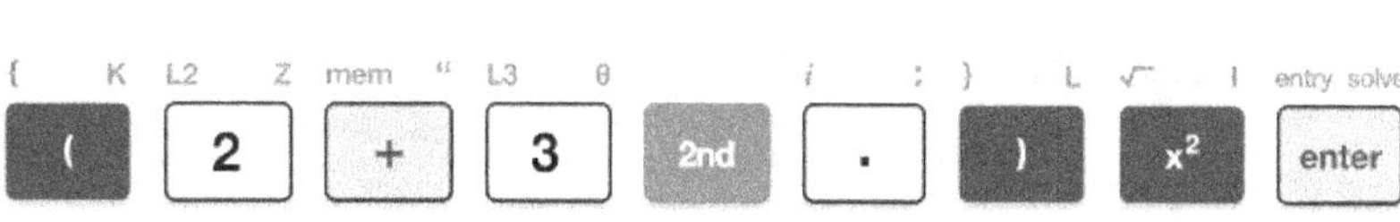

36. Which of the following is equivalent to i^{63} ?

F. $-i$

G. i

H. $63i$

J. -1

K. 1

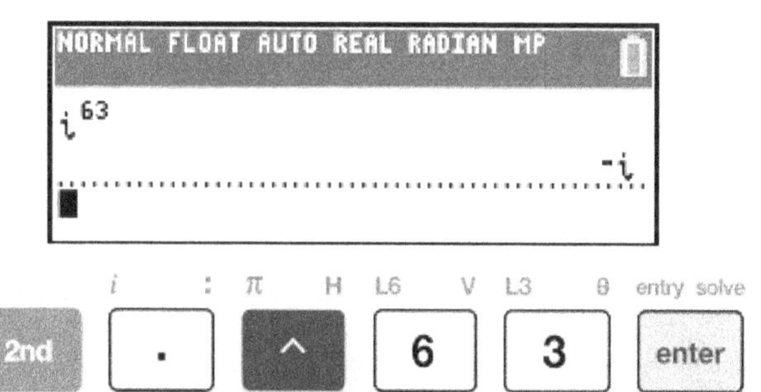

A word of caution with "large" exponents: you may get something that looks different than what you are anticipating.

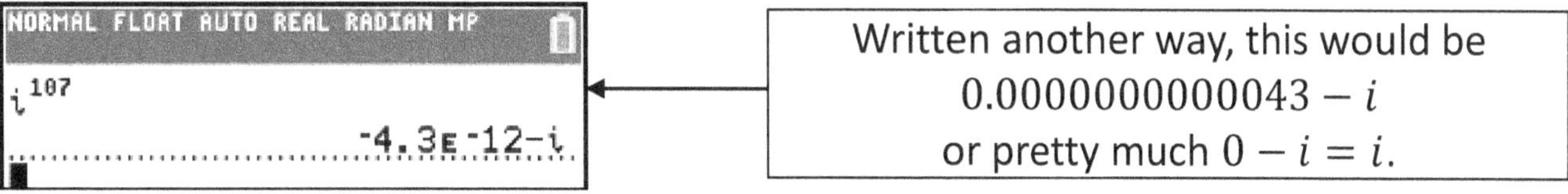

Your calculator isn't really expecting to ever work with an exponent over i that large, so there's some error in how it's calculated.

SCIENTIFIC NOTATION

Speaking of large exponents (or small ones!), we have scientific notation. Like many functions on the calculator, there are a couple ways of working with scientific notation.

1. Using the EE option:

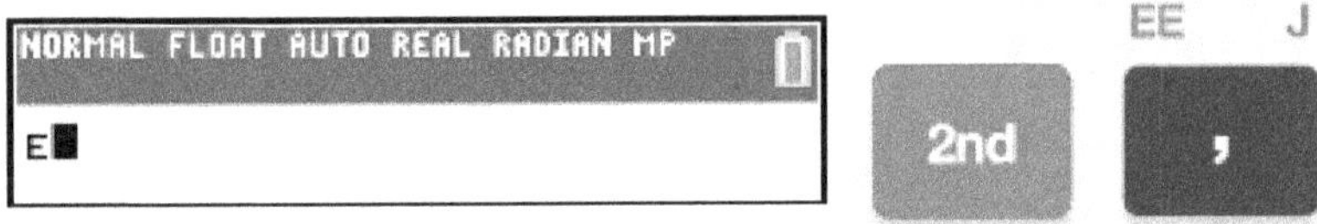

No, I don't know why it is two E on top of the button. Yes, I'm too lazy to Google why.

2. Changing your calculator to **sci** in the mode :

Once you've changed the mode to **sci**, anything on the home screen will be written in scientific notation (kind of).

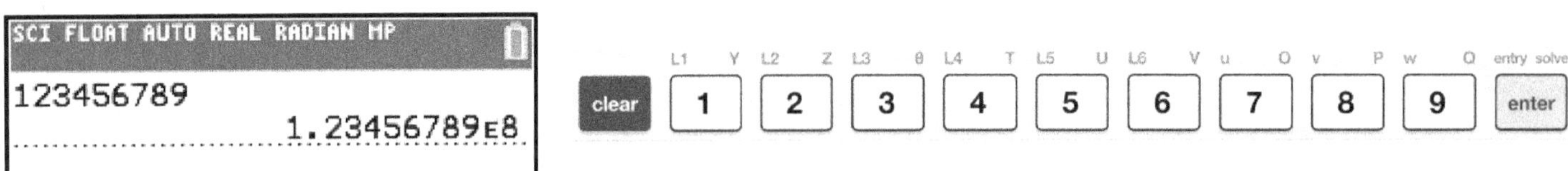

Now, the calculator's scientific notation and what we learn in school are probably different. At this point, you've probably already figured out what the calculator means, but just in case:

Think of E as $10^{\square}$

$$120{,}000 = 1.2 \times 10^5 = 1.2\text{E}5$$

$$0.00419 = 4.19 \times 10^{-3} = 4.19\text{E}{-3}$$

SCIENTIFIC NOTATION

As a general rule, if you're given scientific notation already, the EE option is probably best. If you're trying to convert to scientific notation, being in **sci** mode is probably ideal.

16. In scientific notation,
$314{,}000{,}000 + 810{,}000{,}000 = ?$

> Since you're asked to convert into scientific notation, being in **sci** mode is probably best.

F. 1.124×10^{-10}

G. 1.124×10^{8}

H. 1.124×10^{9}

J. 1.124×10^{10}

K. 1124×10^{10}

12. Which of the following is equivalent to $(4.0 \times 10^{4})(3.7 \times 10^{5})$?

> Since you're already given scientific notation, it's best to use the EE option.

F. 1.48×10^{-10}

G. 1.48×10^{8}

H. 1.48×10^{9}

J. 1.48×10^{10}

K. 14.8×10^{9}

In both the previous questions, you can instantly get rid of the **K** answer since scientific notation can only have one digit to the left of the decimal.

38. The average distance from the Earth to the Sun, which is 9.40×10^{7} miles, is about how many times the average distance from Mercury to the Sun, which is 2.99×10^{6} miles?

> Since you're already given scientific notation, it's best to use the EE option.

F. 3.14×10^{1}

G. 6.41×10^{1}

H. 3.14×10^{13}

J. 1.40×10^{14}

K. 2.81×10^{14}

FOCUSED EXAMPLES

EXAMPLES TO TRY ON YOUR CALCULATOR

Answer

1.	What is the value of $\frac{2}{3} + \frac{5}{7}$? Also, convert your answer to a mixed number.	$\frac{29}{21}$ or $1\frac{8}{21}$
2.	Find the value of $\frac{3}{4}\left(\frac{1}{2} - \frac{2}{3}\right)$.	$-\frac{1}{8}$
3.	Find the value of $5\frac{2}{5} - 1\frac{2}{3}$; write answer as both a mixed number and improper fraction.	$\frac{56}{15}$ or $3\frac{11}{15}$
4.	Find the value of $\lvert -3 + 7 \rvert - \lvert 2 - 8 \rvert$.	-2
5.	Find the value of $5 \times \left\lvert \frac{3}{8} - \frac{4}{7} \right\rvert$.	$-\frac{55}{56}$
6.	Find the value of $\frac{2 \times \lvert -2 - 7 \rvert + 1}{8 \div 4 + 1}$; write answer as both a mixed number and improper fraction.	$\frac{19}{3}$ or $6\frac{1}{3}$
7.	Find the value of $\frac{x}{2y} + xy$ if $x = 3$ and $y = -4$.	$-\frac{99}{8}$ or $-12\frac{3}{8}$
8.	Find the value of $\lvert a - b \rvert - \lvert b - a \rvert$ if $a = -1$ and $b = 2$.	0
9.	Use NUMERIC SOLVER to find the value of x if $\frac{4}{3}(2x - 1) = 5$.	$\frac{19}{8}$ or 2.375
10.	Use NUMERIC SOLVER to find the value of x if $\frac{2x+1}{3} = \frac{3x-2}{4}$.	10

FOCUSED EXAMPLES

EXAMPLES TO TRY ON YOUR CALCULATOR

		Answer
1.	What is $\sqrt[4]{81}$?	**3**
2.	What is $\sqrt[5]{1024}$?	**4**
3.	What is $\sqrt[3]{\dfrac{1}{8}}$?	$\dfrac{1}{2}$
4.	What is $(2 - 3i)(2 + 3i)$?	**13**
5.	If the product of x and $5 - 4i$ is 31, what is the value of x? (Hint: divide 31 by $5 - 4i$)	$5 + 4i$
6.	What is $(2 + 7i)^2$?	$-45 + 28i$
7.	What is the value of i^{44} ?	**1**
8.	Write 0.000000137 in scientific notation.	$1.37\text{E}{-}7$
9.	What is $267{,}000 + 912{,}000$ in scientific notation?	$1.179\text{E}6$
10.	What is $(2.2 \times 10^7)(6.8 \times 10^4)$ in scientific notation?	$1.496\text{E}12$
11.	What is $\dfrac{8.1 \times 10^{-7}}{2.7 \times 10^5}$ in scientific notation?	$3.0\text{E}{-}12$

www.TestPrepWizards.com

LCM and GCF

Two of the more confused terms by students are **factors** and **multiples**. For *multiples*, think of *multipl*ying or, better yet, a multiplication table.

Suppose you wanted to find the multiples of 8. If you break out that ol' school composition notebook, the back cover should have a multiplication table.

	1	2	3	4	5	6	7	8	9	10	11	12
1	1	2	3	4	5	6	7	8	9	10	11	12
2	2	4	6	8	10	12	14	16	18	20	22	24
3	3	6	9	12	15	18	21	24	27	30	33	36
4	4	8	12	16	20	24	28	32	36	40	44	48
5	5	10	15	20	25	30	35	40	45	50	55	60
6	6	12	18	24	30	36	42	48	54	60	66	72
7	7	14	21	28	35	42	49	56	63	70	77	84
8	8	16	24	32	40	48	56	64	72	80	88	96	← Multiples of 8
9	9	18	27	36	45	54	63	72	81	90	99	108
10	10	20	30	40	50	60	70	80	90	100	110	120
11	11	22	33	44	55	66	77	88	99	110	121	132
12	12	24	36	48	60	72	84	96	108	120	132	144

The multiples of 8 are the numbers that appear, or would appear, in the 8 row.

On the other hand, any integer which divides evenly into another number is a factor. Therefore, an integer is always **divisible** by its factors.

For instance, the factors of 20 are 1, 2, 4, 5, 10, and 20 since 20 is divisible by 1, 2, 4, 5, 10, and 20. Technically, multiples and factors can also be negative, but that's sort of swept under the rug on the ACT.

The **least common multiple** (LCM) of two or more numbers is the smallest multiple that those two or more numbers share. Questions about **least common denominators** are many times just LCM questions.

To find the LCM on the calculator:

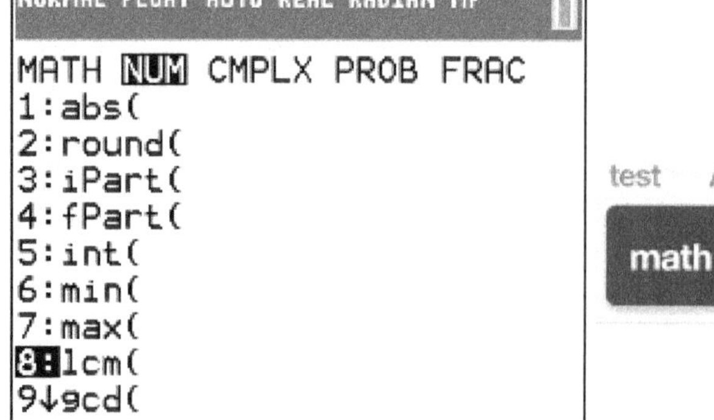

LCM and GCF

The LCM has two arguments that it needs to work—two numbers.

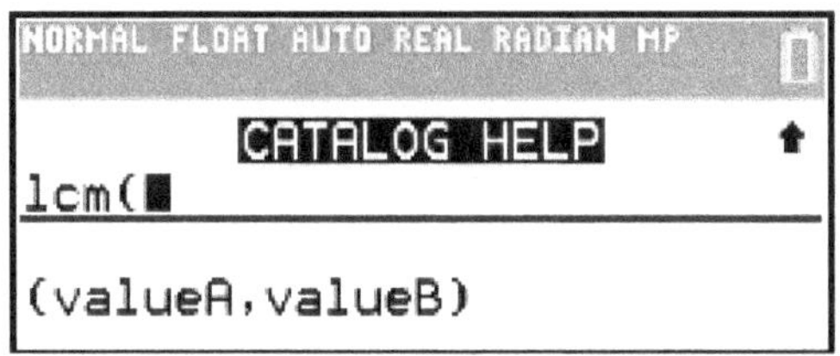

We'll either see this "two numbers only" shortcoming can be overcome with programs (check out our website!) or with nested LCM functions.

Similarly, the greatest common factor, **GCD** on the calculator, is in a similar spot and has the same "two number only" shortcoming.

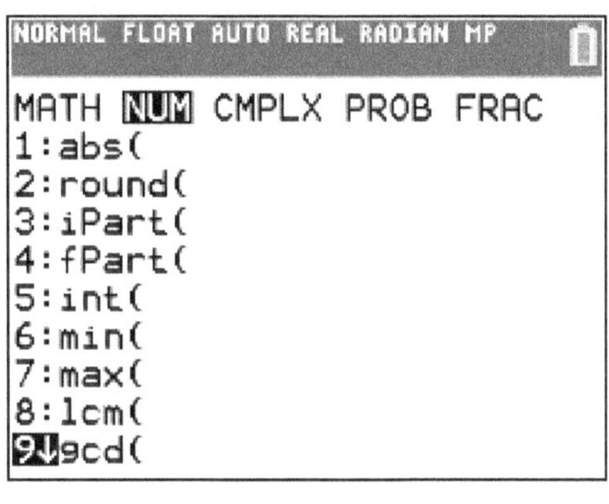

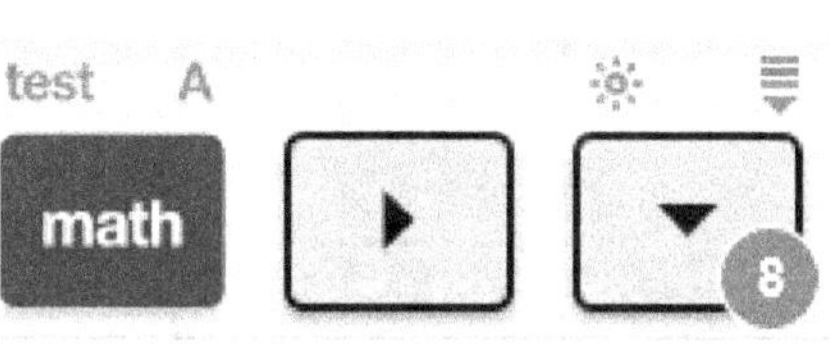

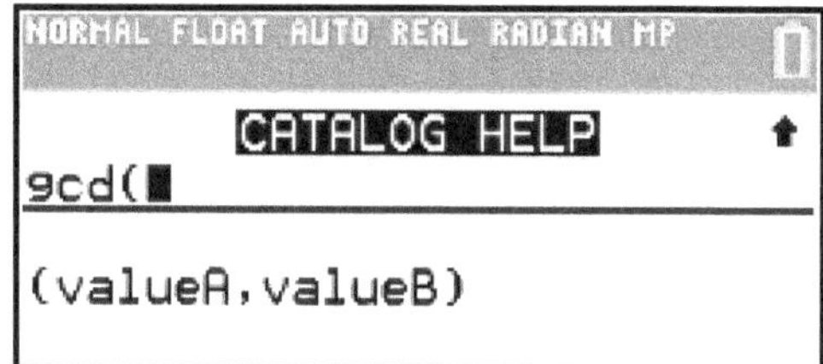

6. What is the least common multiple of 6 and 8 ?

- **F.** 2
- **G.** 6
- **H.** 14
- **J.** 24
- **K.** 48

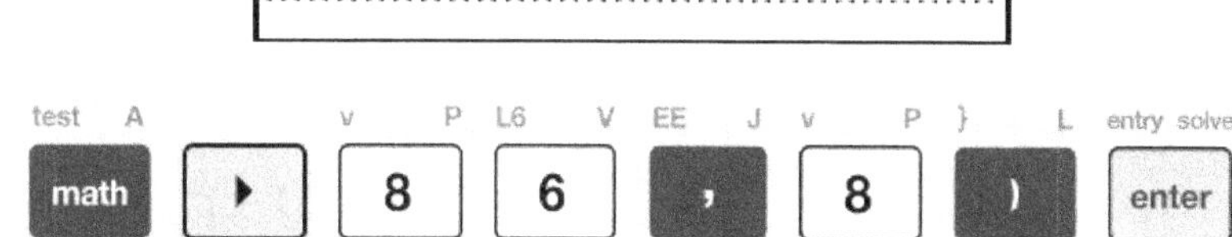

In case you've lost it, the comma is one button above 7 .

14. 28 and 70 are both divisible by some integer, x. What is the largest value of x ?

- **F.** 7
- **G.** 14
- **H.** 52
- **J.** 98
- **K.** 280

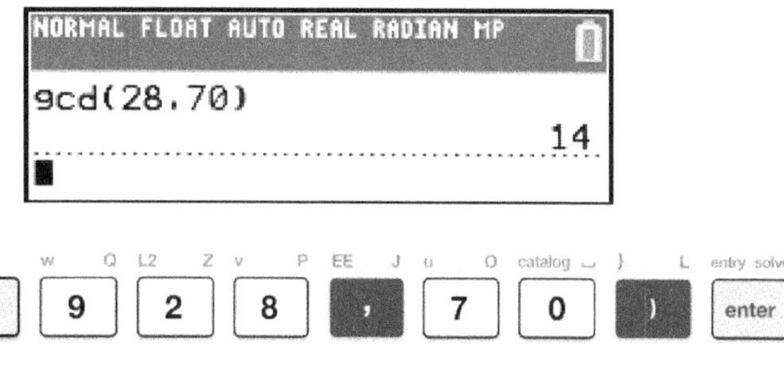

LCM and GCF

Nesting functions means placing one function inside of another. Since the **LCM** and **GCD** only allow for two numbers in their arguments, you'll need to nest another **LCM** (or **GCD**, but it's unlikely on the ACT) inside your first **LCM**.

14. What is the least common multiple of 6, 8, and 9 ?

F. 1

G. 24

H. 54

J. 72

K. 432

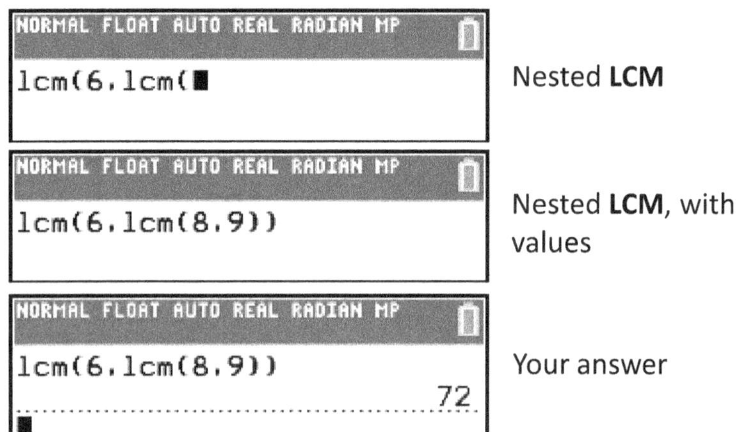

There's really no limit to the number of nested **LCM** you can have (computer science geeks, please don't email me and talk about the memory limits of the calculator). I've seen six—count 'em—SIX numbers in a least common multiple question on the ACT. Granted, it only happened once…and that was 2004 (April to be exact), but just in case…

32. What is the least common multiple of 2, 3, 4, 5, 8, and 12 ?

F. 1

G. 96

H. 120

J. 5,760

K. 11,520

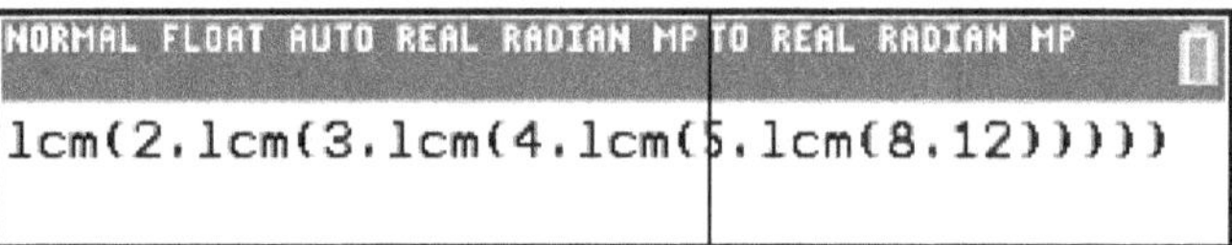

Hey, it doesn't fit on the calculator screen. What do you want us to do?

Remember, finding a least common denominator is the same as finding a least common multiple. This question has the same approach (and answer) as question 14 from above.

18. What is the least common denominator of $\frac{1}{6}, \frac{1}{8},$ and $\frac{1}{9}$?

F. 1

G. 24

H. 54

J. 72

K. 432

REMAINDERS

Remainders, on their own, do not appear on the ACT, per se. That is, as of this writing, you will not be asked something like, "What is the remainder when 93 is divided by 7?"

Why do we care about remainders then? Because most *pattern* questions can be (and should be) solved with remainders. Pattern questions may look like the following:

36. Santosh is creating a mosaic by laying colored tiles in the following pattern: Red, Blue, Green, Yellow, Orange, Red, Blue, Green, Yellow, Orange, and so on. If Santosh continues this pattern, what will be the color of the 812th tile?

    F. Red

    G. Blue

    H. Green

    J. Yellow

    K. Orange

18. In the decimal expansion of $\frac{2}{7}$, what is the 491st digit to the right of the decimal point?

Note: $\frac{2}{7} = 0.285714285714\ldots$

    F. 1

    G. 2

    H. 4

    J. 5

    K. 7

To solve a pattern question that involves some stupid number of terms (like 812 or 491 as in the questions above), there are three steps:

1. Find the number of terms in the pattern.
2. Find the remainder when the stupidly large term (**dividend**) is divided by the number of terms in the pattern (**divisor**).
3. Find what value in your pattern corresponds to your remainder.

The **remainder** function on your calculators is nuzzling up with the **LCM** and **GCF**. It, too, has two arguments.

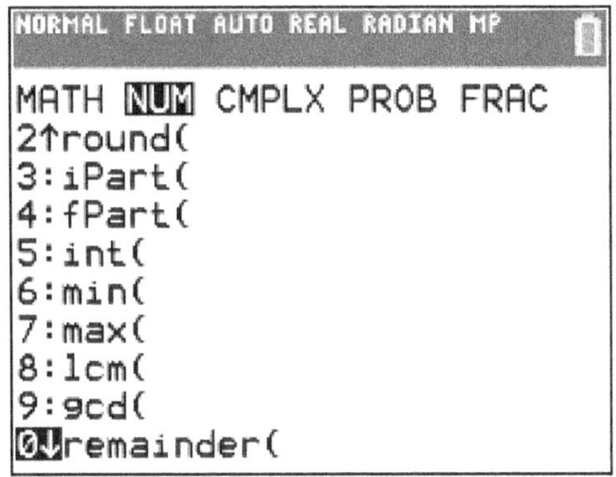

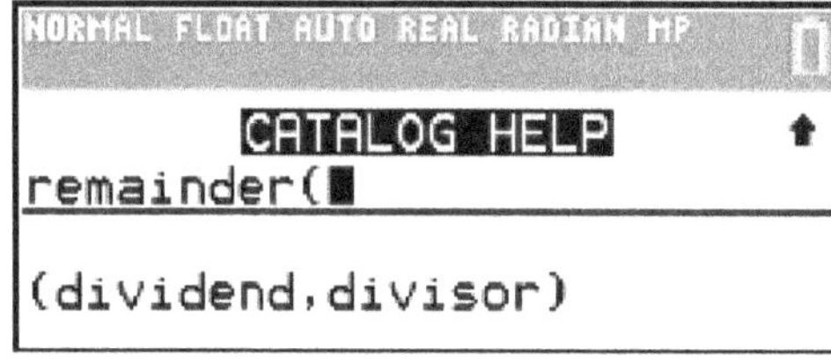

REMAINDERS

So, for the following questions:

36. Santosh is creating a mosaic by laying colored tiles in the following pattern: Red, Blue, Green, Yellow, Orange, Red, Blue, Green, Yellow, Orange, and so on. If Santosh continues this pattern, what will be the color of the 812th tile?

   F. Red

   G. Blue

   H. Green

   J. Yellow

   K. Orange

18. In the decimal expansion of $\frac{2}{7}$, what is the 491st digit to the right of the decimal point?

Note: $\frac{2}{7} = 0.285714285714\ldots$

   F. 1

   G. 2

   H. 4

   J. 5

   K. 7

Number of terms in pattern: (Divisor)	5
	Red, Blue, Green, Yellow, Orange
Stupid Term: (Dividend)	812

```
NORMAL FLOAT AUTO REAL RADIAN MP

remainder(812,5)
                              2
```

Number of terms in pattern: (Divisor)	6
	The 2, 8, 5, 7, 1, and 4
Stupid Term: (Dividend)	491

```
NORMAL FLOAT AUTO REAL RADIAN MP

remainder(491,6)
                              5
```

Since the remainder is <u>2</u>, find the <u>2</u>nd term in the pattern:

   Red, Blue, Green, Yellow, Orange

Since the remainder is <u>5</u>, find the <u>5</u>th term in the pattern:

   2, 8, 5, 7, 1, 4

Sometimes, you have to find the pattern yourself—on recent ACT exams, this is usually a number raised to a ridiculous exponent. These questions will almost certainly be question number 40 or higher: a difficult question.

EXAMPLE: What digit is in the unit place (one's digit) of 2^{1237} ?

Writing out the powers of 2:
$2^1 = 2$
$2^2 = 4$
$2^3 = 8$
$2^4 = 16$
$2^5 = 32$
$2^6 = 64$
$2^7 = 128$
$\vdots$

Every 4 terms, the units digit repeats!

```
NORMAL FLOAT AUTO REAL RADIAN MP

remainder(1237,4)
                              1
```

So, 2^{1237} will have the same unit digit as 2^1, or simply 2.

REMAINDERS

A word of caution with remainders—if the remainder is ever 0, **your answer is the _last_ term in your pattern**. Many students mistakenly think this means the first term in the pattern. When you have a remainder of 0, it means that your dividend was divisible by the divisor. Look at that alliteration in a math book!

42. At a town parade, the floats have a specified number of balloons. The first float has 12 balloons, the second float has 8 balloons, the third float has 7 balloons, and the fourth float has 2 balloons. For every float after the fourth, the pattern starts again: 12 balloons on the fifth float, 8 balloons on the sixth float, 7 balloons on the seventh float, and 2 balloons on the eight float. If this pattern continues, how many balloons will be on the 88th float?

Number of terms in pattern: (Divisor)	4 12, 8, 7, and 2
Stupid Term (Dividend)	88

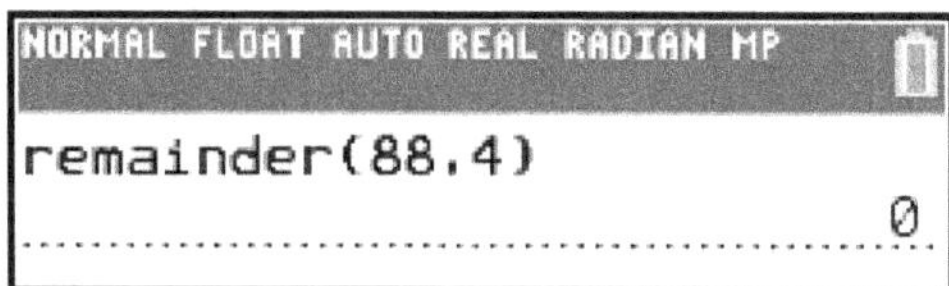

Since the remainder is 0, find the _LAST_ term in the pattern:

$$12, 8, 7, 2$$

- **F.** 2
- **G.** 7
- **H.** 8
- **J.** 12
- **K.** Cannot be determined

FOCUSED EXAMPLES

EXAMPLES TO TRY ON YOUR CALCULATOR

Answer

1.	What is the greatest common factor of 21 and 98 ?	7
2.	What is the greatest common factor of 108 and 72 ?	36
3.	What is the least common multiple of 15 and 10 ?	30
4.	What is the least common multiple of 4, 9, and 12 ?	36
5.	What is the least common multiple of 8, 12, and 18 ?	72
6.	What is the least common denominator of $\frac{1}{5}, \frac{3}{6}$, and $\frac{7}{8}$?	120
7.	One light blinks every 16 seconds and another light blinks every 6 seconds. If the two lights blink at the same time, how many seconds pass before they next blink at the same time?	48
8.	What is the 517th digit to the right of the decimal point in $0.\overline{076923}$?	1
9.	What is the $2{,}790^{th}$ letter in the pattern TPWTPWTPW …?	W
10.	What digit is in the units place (ones digit) of 7^{35} ?	3
11.	What digit is in the units place (ones digit) of 3^{248}?	1

MATRICES

Matrices (singular: matrix) are one of the topics on the ACT that are occurring with more frequency. In our experience, matrices fall under a weird region in high school curriculums. Some students I work with have never seen them, and some students see them early on in Algebra 2.

So long as you can recognize the types of matrix questions that the calculator can handle, you're fine for the ACT.

A matrix is an array of values organized into rows and columns. For instance, the matrix below is a two by three matrix because there are two rows and three columns. It's important to understand that we *always* describe matrices first by their rows, then by their columns.

$$\begin{bmatrix} 2 & 3 & -1 \\ 0 & 17 & 2.7 \end{bmatrix}$$

A matrix may also contain variables or expressions. Below is a two by two matrix (known as a **square matrix** because the rows and columns are the same) with variables and expressions.

$$\begin{bmatrix} x & x + 2y \\ 3z & z - x \end{bmatrix}$$

Since this isn't a "teach you the ACT math" book, all I'm going to do is show you how to use the **matrix** button on your calculator.

1. Using the secondary option **matrix** on $\boxed{x^{-1}}$:

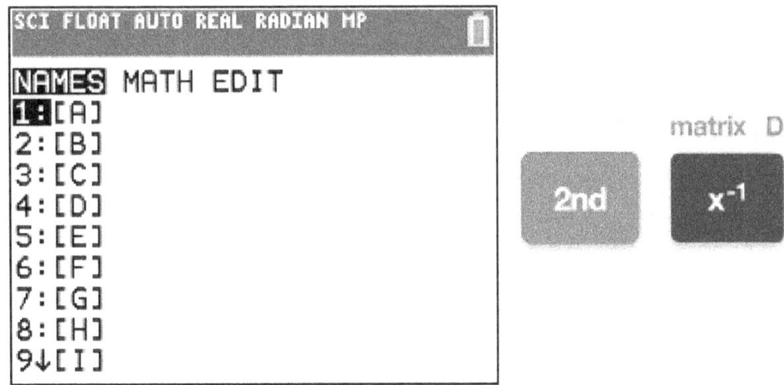

Using this method will require us to name matrices and then recall them. Yuck.

MATRICES

Most people who learn matrices in school (and are allowed to use calculators) use this option. **I strongly suggest you actually use the following method for matrices on the calculator.**

2. The **mtrx** option in the secret menu:

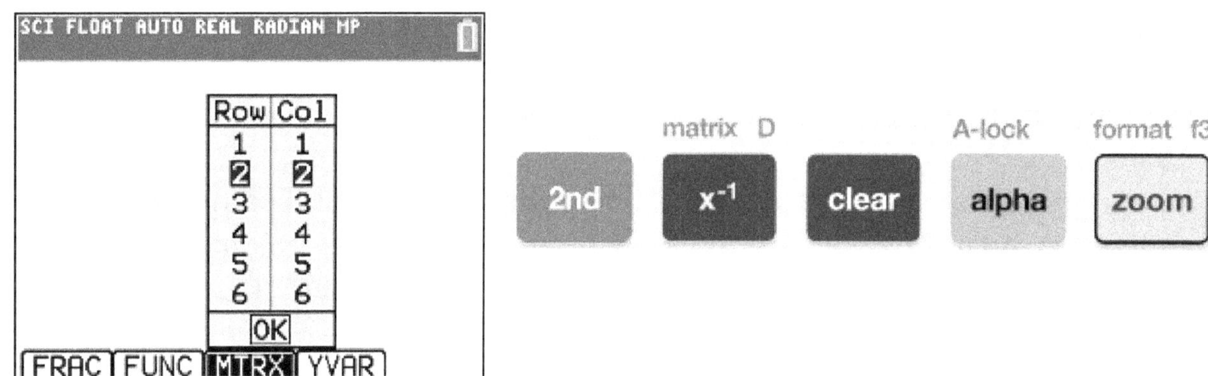

This is the *only* way to actually put a matrix template on your home screen. Being able to match what you see on the home screen to the question on the page ensures that you are not about to make a mistake.

32. Matrices A and B are given below.

$$A = \begin{bmatrix} 2 & -1 \\ 5 & 6 \end{bmatrix} \quad B = \begin{bmatrix} -4 & 3 \\ 1 & 2 \end{bmatrix}$$

Which of the following matrices is $A - B$?

F. $\begin{bmatrix} -6 & 4 \\ 6 & 8 \end{bmatrix}$

G. $\begin{bmatrix} -2 & -1 \\ 5 & 6 \end{bmatrix}$

H. $\begin{bmatrix} -2 & 2 \\ 6 & 8 \end{bmatrix}$

J. $\begin{bmatrix} 6 & 3 \\ 11 & 1 \end{bmatrix}$

K. $\begin{bmatrix} 6 & -4 \\ 4 & 4 \end{bmatrix}$

We're going to have to put 2 two by two matrices on the home screen.

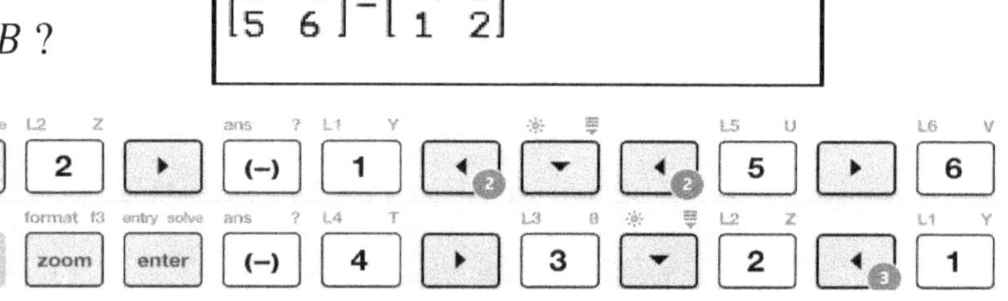

Once again, it looks like a ton of key strokes, but the majority of them are moving around in the matrix to input your values.

MATRICES

You can also multiply a matrix by a value along with matrix operations.

16.
$$3\begin{bmatrix} 2 & 4 \\ 1 & 3 \end{bmatrix} + 4\begin{bmatrix} 1 & 0 \\ -2 & -1 \end{bmatrix} = ?$$

F. $\begin{bmatrix} 3 & 4 \\ -1 & 2 \end{bmatrix}$

G. $\begin{bmatrix} 3 & 4 \\ 3 & 4 \end{bmatrix}$

H. $\begin{bmatrix} 10 & 12 \\ -5 & 5 \end{bmatrix}$

J. $\begin{bmatrix} 18 & 4 \\ 12 & -12 \end{bmatrix}$

K. $\begin{bmatrix} 21 & 28 \\ 7 & 14 \end{bmatrix}$

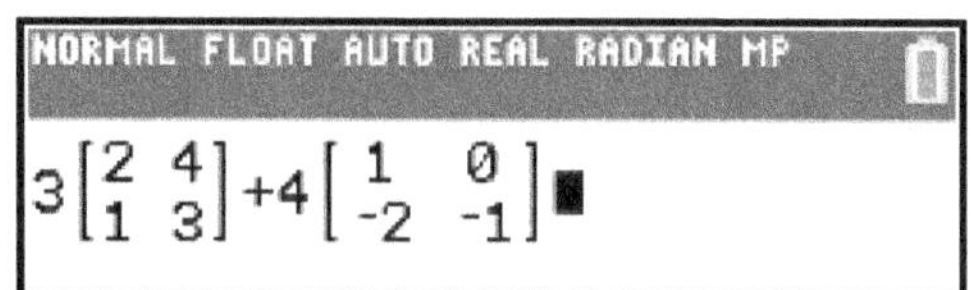

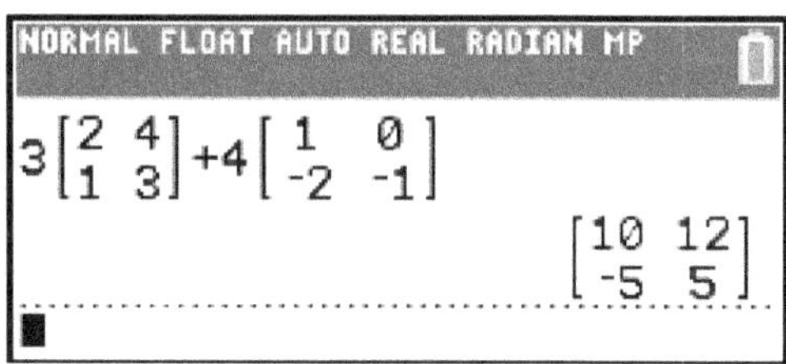

You can change the dimensions of a matrix in the **mtrx** option by scrolling to the correct number of rows, pressing [enter], scrolling to the correct number of columns, pressing [enter], and then hitting OK (press [enter]). This is common for matrix multiplication questions.

52.
$$\begin{bmatrix} 3 & -4 \\ -2 & 2 \end{bmatrix} \cdot \begin{bmatrix} 5 \\ -3 \end{bmatrix} = ?$$

F. $\begin{bmatrix} 15 & -20 \\ -10 & -6 \end{bmatrix}$

G. $\begin{bmatrix} 15 & -12 \\ -10 & -6 \end{bmatrix}$

H. $\begin{bmatrix} 8 & 1 \\ -5 & -1 \end{bmatrix}$

J. $\begin{bmatrix} 3 \\ -4 \end{bmatrix}$

K. $\begin{bmatrix} 27 \\ -16 \end{bmatrix}$

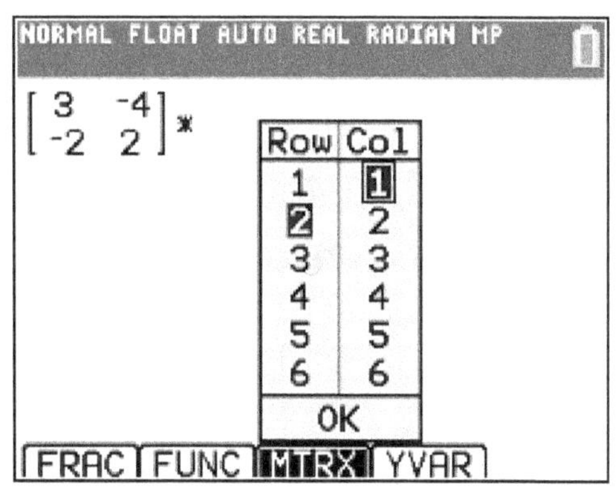

Put in first matrix, then put in a two row by 1 column matrix.

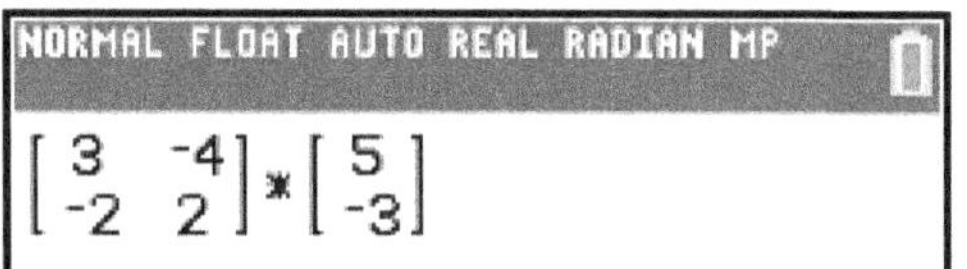

Input values for second matrix.

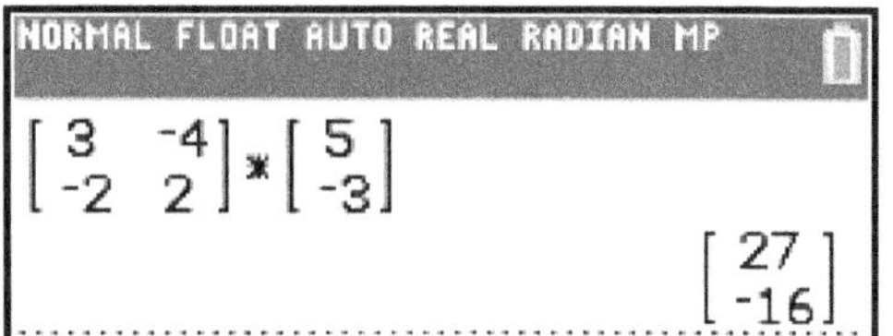

Revel in the ease of finding your answer.

www.TestPrepWizards.com

MATRICES

Yet another word of caution: **matrix multiplication is NOT commutative.** That is, the order that you input the matrices matters. If you flip 'em in the previous question, chaos ensues.

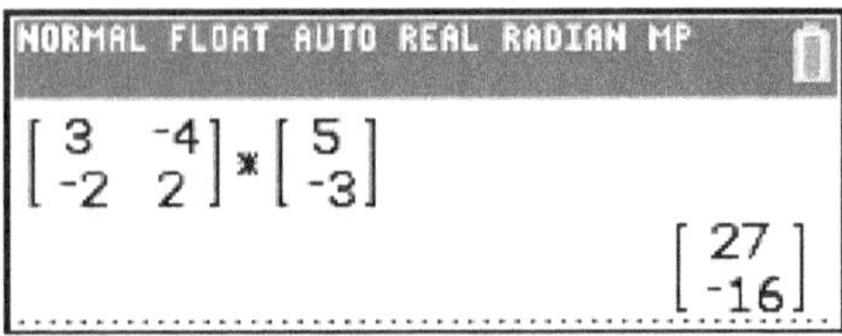 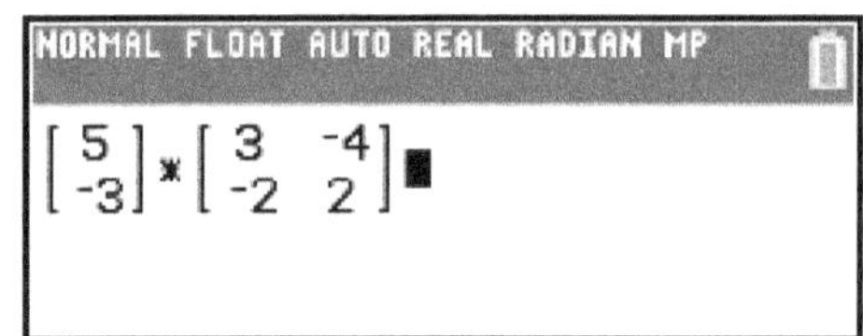 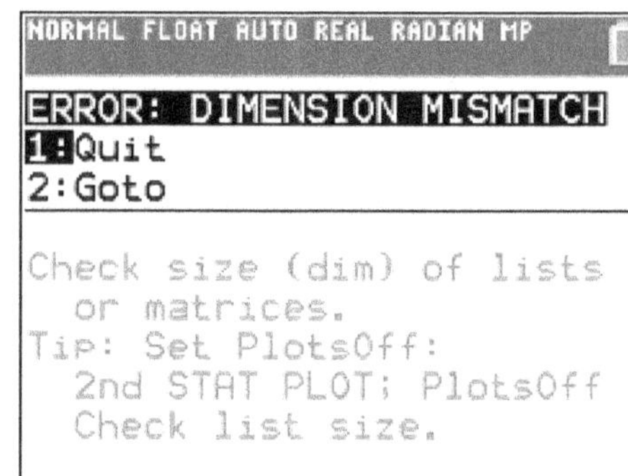

This is due to the way matrix multiplication is defined. You cannot multiply matrices unless *the columns of the first matrix equal the rows of the second matrix.*

The last matrix concept that we can do on our calculator is calculating the **determinant**. For starters, you can only find the determinant of a square matrix (equal number of rows and columns).

It is highly unlikely that the ACT would ever expect you to find the determinant of anything other than a two by two matrix.

To find the determinant:

1. Access the **matrix** option by pressing 2nd x^{-1}

2. Scroll to the **MATH** option, then press [enter] on **det(**
3. Input your matrix and press [enter]

54. What is the determinant of the matrix shown below?

$$\begin{vmatrix} 5 & 1 \\ -2 & -4 \end{vmatrix}$$

F. 17

G. 13

H. 0

J. −18

K. −22

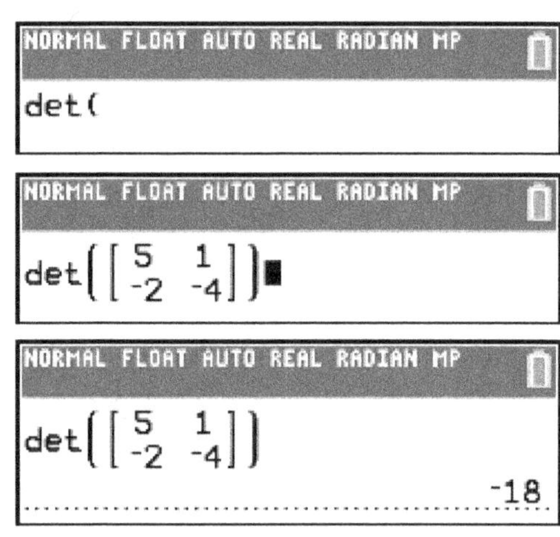

FOCUSED EXAMPLES

EXAMPLES TO TRY ON YOUR CALCULATOR

Answer

1. What is $\begin{bmatrix} 1 & 2 \\ 9 & 8 \end{bmatrix} + \begin{bmatrix} 4 & -1 \\ -3 & 5 \end{bmatrix}$?

$\begin{bmatrix} 5 & 1 \\ 6 & 13 \end{bmatrix}$

2. What is $2\begin{bmatrix} 1 & 3 \\ -1 & 2 \end{bmatrix} - 4\begin{bmatrix} 6 & 3 \\ -1 & 0 \end{bmatrix}$?

$\begin{bmatrix} -22 & -6 \\ 2 & 4 \end{bmatrix}$

3. What is $\begin{bmatrix} 1 & 2 \\ 3 & 4 \end{bmatrix} \cdot \begin{bmatrix} -1 & 3 \\ -4 & 2 \end{bmatrix}$?

$\begin{bmatrix} -9 & 7 \\ -19 & 17 \end{bmatrix}$

4. What is $\begin{bmatrix} 4 \\ 5 \\ 6 \end{bmatrix} \cdot \begin{bmatrix} 1 & 2 & 3 \end{bmatrix}$?

$\begin{bmatrix} 4 & 8 & 12 \\ 5 & 10 & 15 \\ 6 & 12 & 18 \end{bmatrix}$

5. What is $\begin{bmatrix} 1 & 2 & 3 \end{bmatrix} \cdot \begin{bmatrix} 4 \\ 5 \\ 6 \end{bmatrix}$?

$[32]$

6. What is $\begin{bmatrix} 1 & 2 \\ 3 & 4 \end{bmatrix} \cdot \begin{bmatrix} 5 \\ 6 \end{bmatrix}$?

$\begin{bmatrix} 17 \\ 39 \end{bmatrix}$

7. What is $\begin{bmatrix} 5 \\ 6 \end{bmatrix} \cdot \begin{bmatrix} 1 & 2 \\ 3 & 4 \end{bmatrix}$?

Undefined

8. Find the determinant of $\begin{vmatrix} 1 & -1 \\ -2 & 10 \end{vmatrix}$.

12

9. Use NUMERIC SOLVER to find the value of x such that the determinant of $\begin{vmatrix} 1 & 2 \\ x & 10 \end{vmatrix}$ is equal to 4.

3

10. Use NUMERIC SOLVER to find the <u>positive</u> value of x such that the determinant of $\begin{vmatrix} x & 4 \\ -1 & x \end{vmatrix}$ is equal to 29.

3

OCCASIONALLY USEFUL STUFF—STATISTICS

Let me not be misunderstood—statistics are *very useful.* After all, I am a Statistics professor. However, doing statistics on the calculator tends to be time inefficient for the ACT.

To calculate a **median** (the middle value in an ordered list) and/or the **average** (the sum of all the values divided by the number of values you have):

1. Put your values in a list by pressing $\boxed{\text{stat}}$, pressing $\boxed{\text{enter}}$ on **EDIT**, and then inputting your numbers.

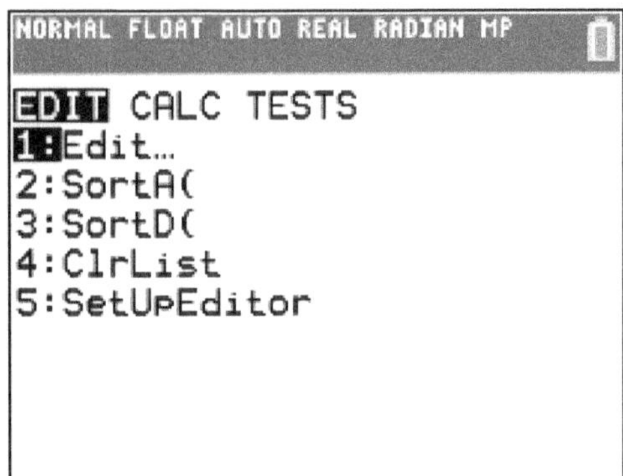 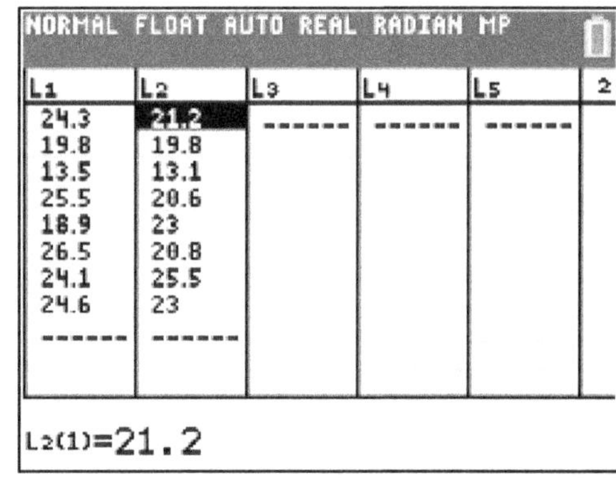

NOTE: If you have values in a list already (like I do), you can scroll to the L_1 or whatever list you want to clear and press $\boxed{\text{clear}}\ \boxed{\text{enter}}$.

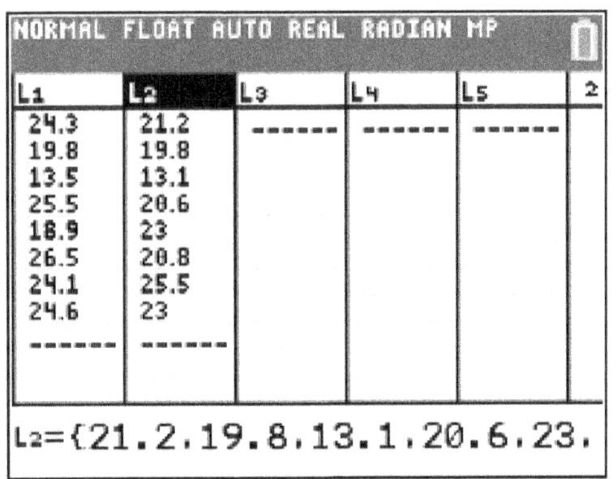 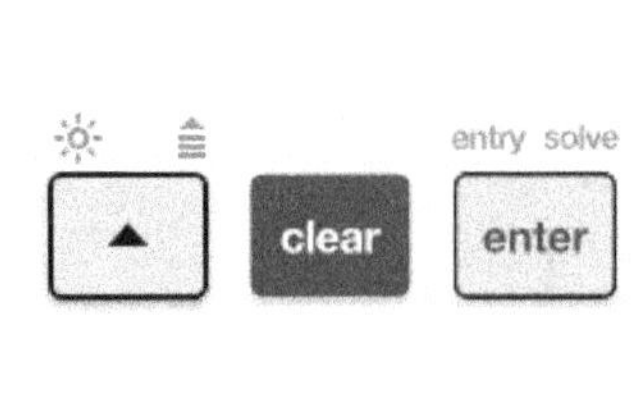 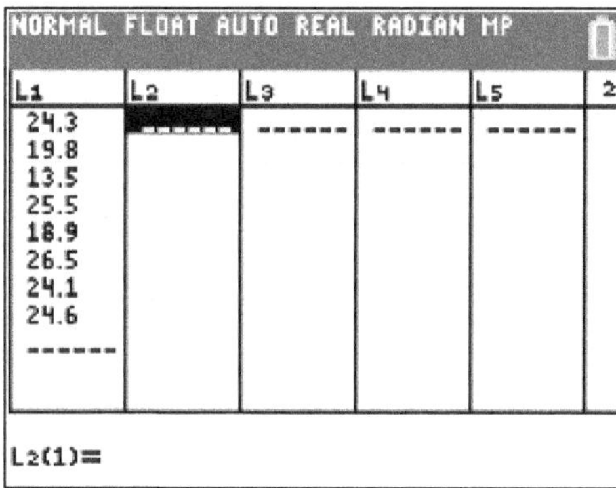

SECOND NOTE: If you have a frequency distribution (explained in a couple of pages), then put the frequencies/counts in L_2.

2. Quit back to the home screen once your values are input.

OCCASIONALLY USEFUL STUFF—STATISTICS

Once the values are successfully input, it's time to actually calculate something. I'm going to put the following 9 values into L_1: 10, 15, 6, 17, 11, 21, 3, 14, 20.

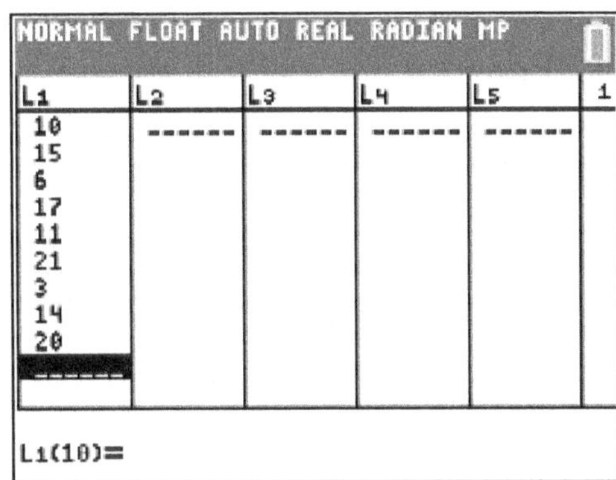

Now, press ⬚stat⬚ and scroll to **CALC**. Use the first option, **1-VAR STATS.**

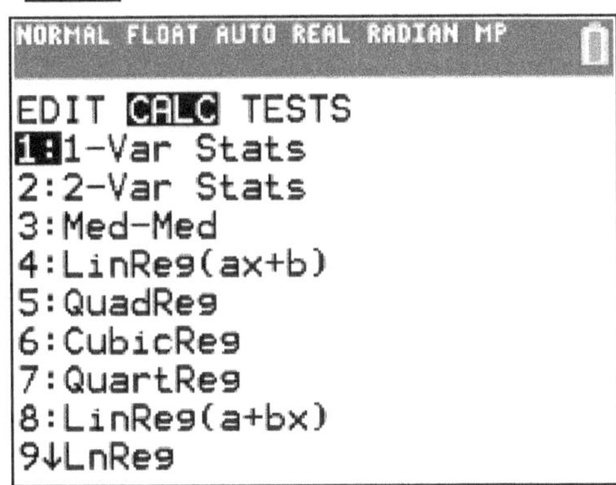

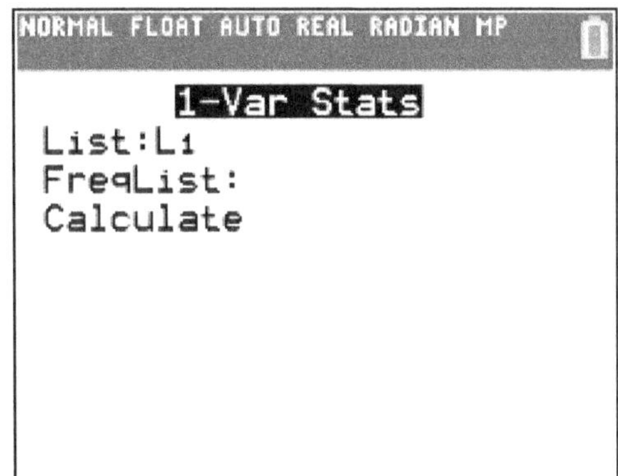

Since we don't have a frequency list, you can just scroll to **Calculate**. NOTE: IF you need to change the **list**, press ⬚**2ⁿᵈ**⬚ ⬚**1 (or 2, 3, 4, 5, or 6)**⬚.

You should get a screen that looks like this:

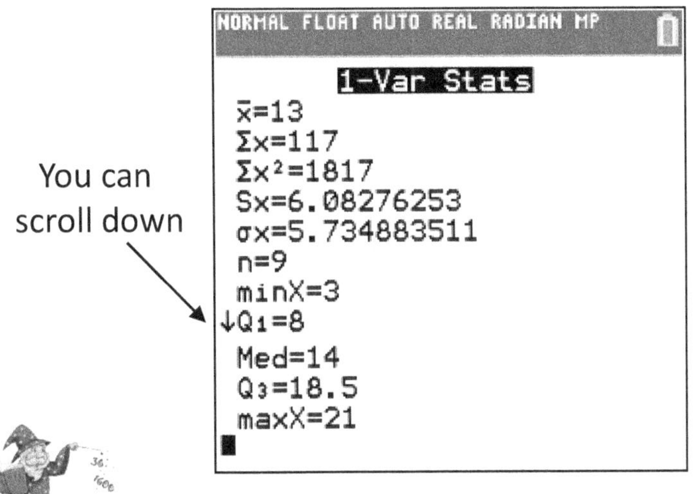

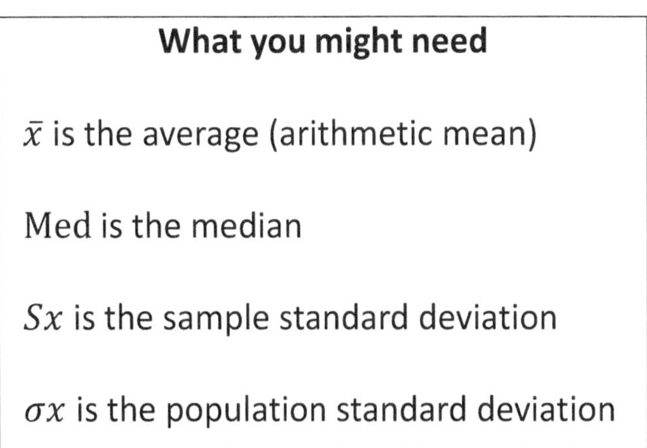

OCCASIONALLY USEFUL STUFF—STATISTICS

For our money, that's a lot of time to spend trying to figure an average or a median. However, when you have a **frequency table,** you can find averages and medians of the entire distribution on the calculator.

32. The table below shows the total number of students in Ms. Kraggle's Chemistry class and how each of those 23 students scored on a national standardized test. What is the average score per student, to the nearest 0.1 point?

Score	Number of students with this score
1	3
2	1
3	4
4	11
5	4

F. 1

G. 2.6

H. 3

J. 3.8

K. 4.6

48. The table below shows the total number of students in Ms. Kraggle's Chemistry class and how each of those 23 students scored on a national standardized test. What is the median score of Ms. Kraggle's students?

Score	Number of students with this score
1	3
2	1
3	4
4	11
5	4

F. 1

G. 2

H. 3

J. 4

K. 5

In this case, we're going to put the left column—the score—into L_1 and the number of occurrences—i.e. the frequency—into L_2.

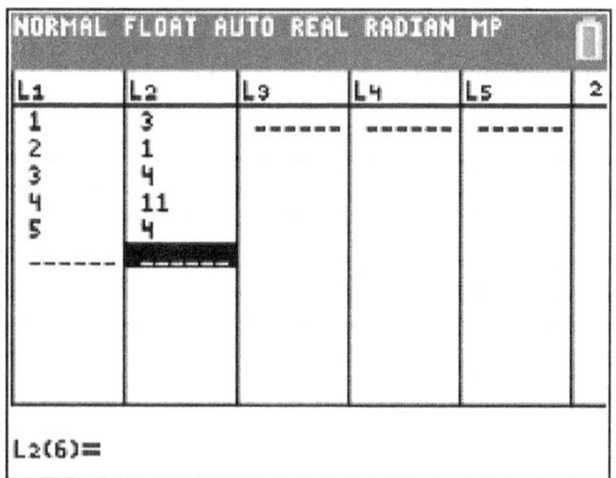

Once we've input our values, quit to the home screen, go back to **1-Var Stats**, and now put L_2 into the **FreqList.**

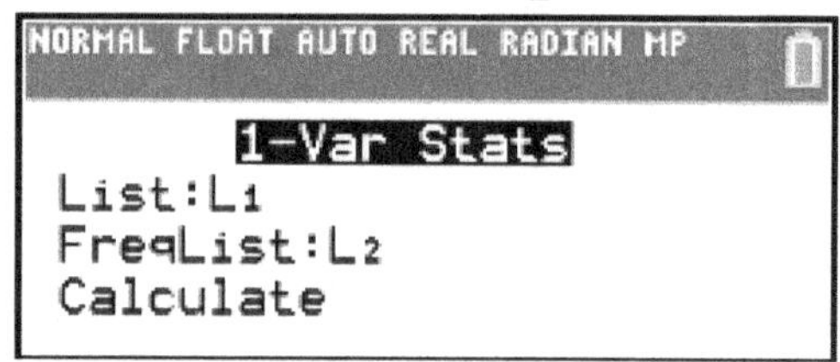

Calculate your values.

(Don't worry, you're not going crazy…

Your screen won't look like this because I cropped out the stuff we didn't need).

RARE STUFF—LOGARITHMS

If you have an equation with logarithms, your **NUMERIC SOLVER** still works—you just need to be careful with your bounds or initial guess.

60. For what real value of x, if any, is
$\log_{(x+4)}(x^2 + 8) = 2$ true?

    F. -2

    G. -1

    H. 0

    J. 1

    K. There is no such value of x.

This is a very tough ACT question, but we can use our **NUMERIC SOLVER** with $E1 = \log_{(x+4)}(x^2 + 8)$ and $E2 = 2$.

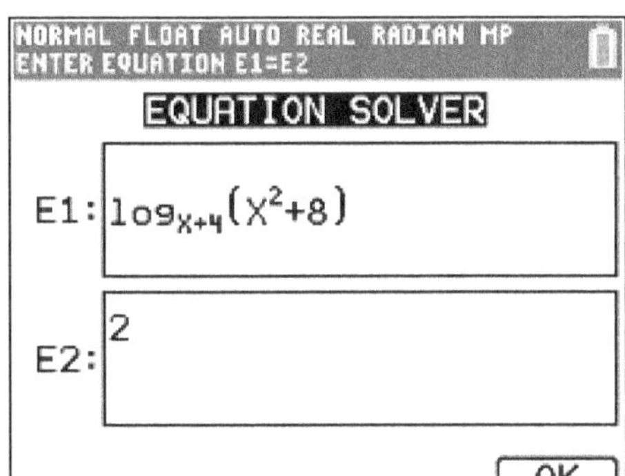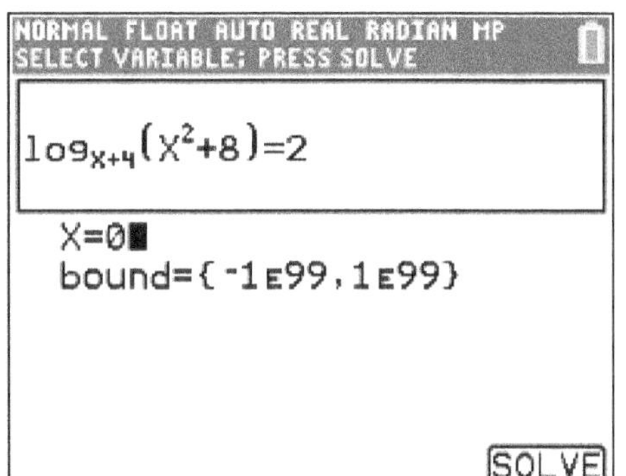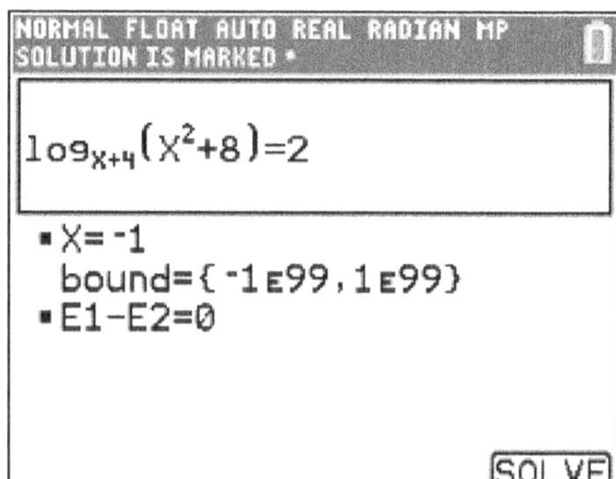

We ran into no issues here because our initial guess of $X = 0$ was near our potential answer choices.

However, suppose we jus threw some random initial guess in—like $X = 20$. Ruh-roh.

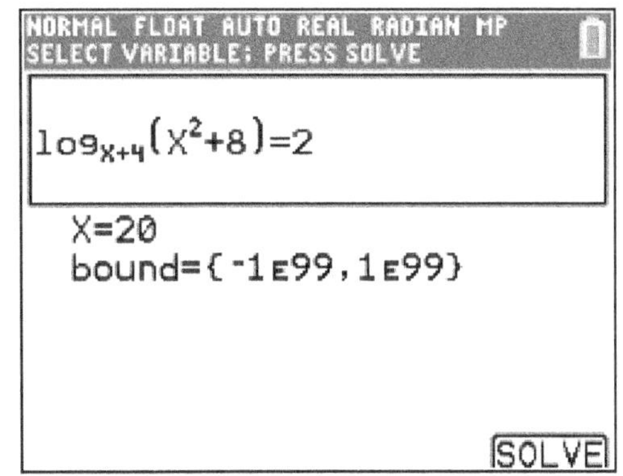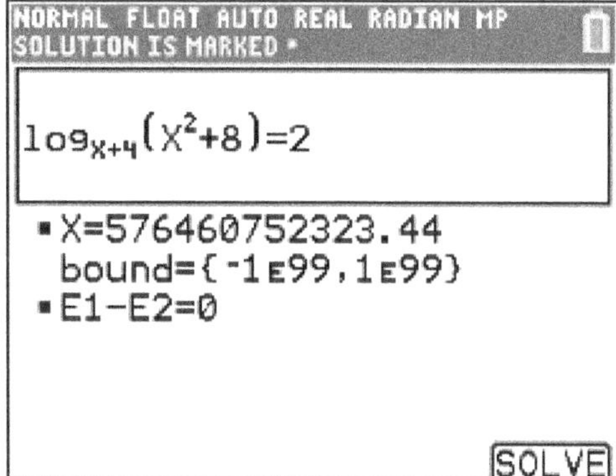

Luckily, 57,6460,752,323.44 wasn't an option. Phew.

RARE STUFF—LOGARITHMS

Logarithms are pretty rare on the ACT. Evaluating logarithms is rarer still. However, you can simplify life on the off chance that a logarithm question appears with the **logbase** function on the calculator. No change of base formula for us rock stars!

1. Using math and the **MATH** option (it's usually option **A**):

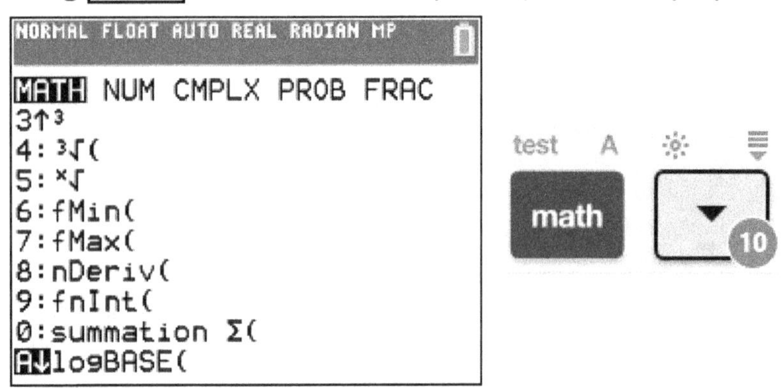

2. The **logbase** option in the secret menu:

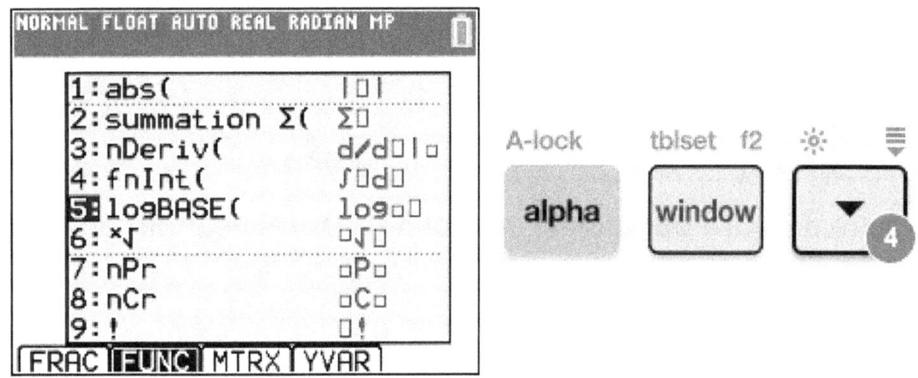

38. What is the value of $\log_3 81$?

F. -4

G. $-\dfrac{1}{4}$

H. $\dfrac{1}{4}$

J. 4

K. 27

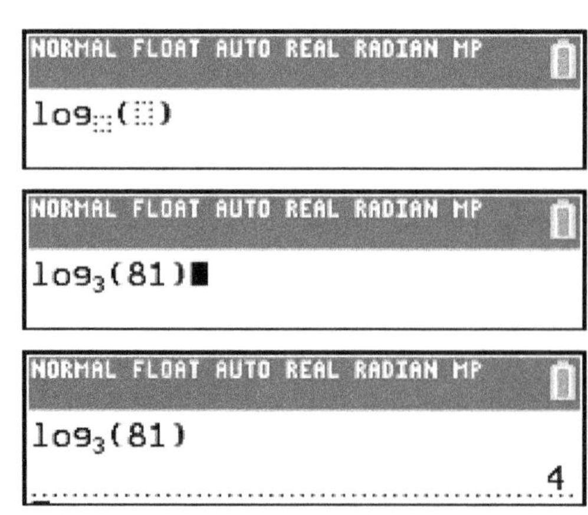

RARE STUFF—FACTORIALS

Much like matrices, some schools districts never cover **factorials**, or $n!$. Students see the exclamation point and be like, "Calm down, n."

A factorial is a notation for multiplication by smaller, positive integers. For instance,

$$5! = 5 \cdot 4 \cdot 3 \cdot 2 \cdot 1 = 120$$

Factorials are super-rare on the test, although it does seem as if they are occurring a bit more often on the latest tests than they did in years past.

1. Using $\boxed{\text{math}}$ and the PROB option. It's the fourth option down:

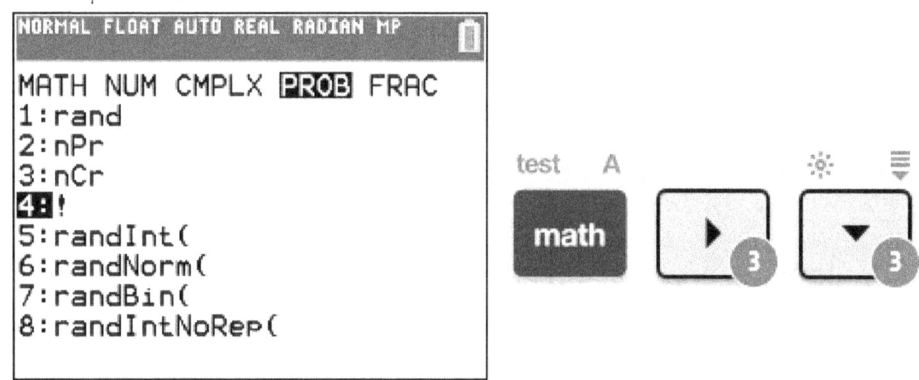

2. The **!** option in the secret menu:

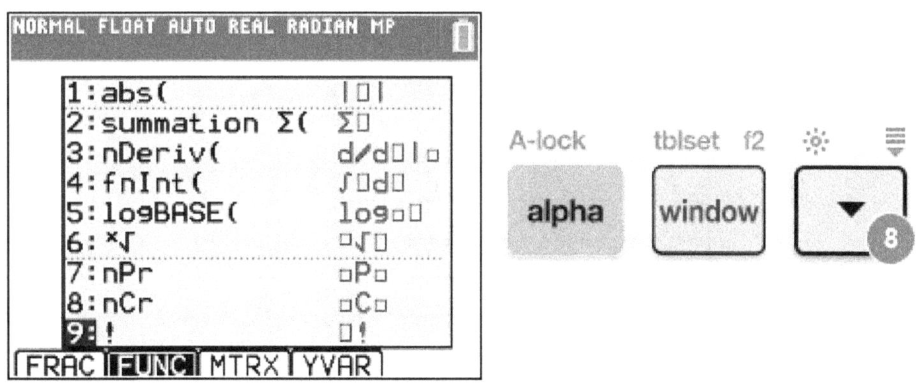

In order to use either one, you need to put a number before the !

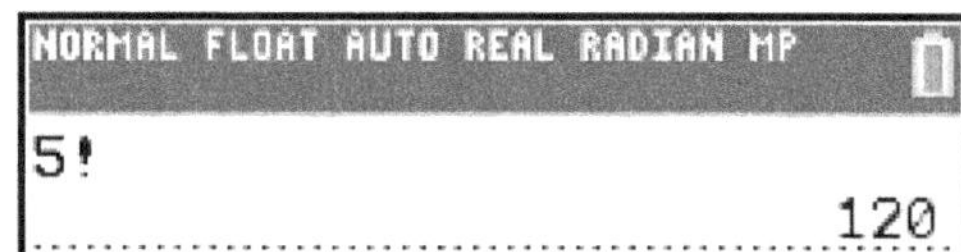

FOCUSED EXAMPLES

EXAMPLES TO TRY ON YOUR CALCULATOR

Answer

1. What is $\log_7 343$?

3

2. What is $\log_4 \left(\dfrac{1}{16}\right)$?

-2

3. Use NUMERIC SOLVER to find the <u>positive</u> value of x that is a solution to $\log_{(x+5)} 36 = 2$. (Hint: Make sure your lower bound is 0)

1

4. What is the value of 6! ?

720

5. What is the value of 7! ?

5040

Use the following information for questions 6 and 7

A new worker is supposed to put three meatballs on every meatball sub that she prepares. However, she kinda just does her own thing. The owner of restaurant randomly chooses 39 sandwiches the worker prepares and counts the number of meatballs on the sub. That information is shown in the table below.

Meatballs on a Sub	Frequency
1	8
2	7
3	1
4	23

6. What is the median number of meatballs on the 39 subs prepared by the new worker?

4

7. What is the average (arithmetic mean) number of meatballs on the 39 subs prepared by the new worker? Round to the nearest tenth of a meatball.

3.0

APPendix A: APPS

Not all apps come preloaded on calculators. However, the three apps here (Conics, Inequalz, and PlySmlt2) are pretty standard. Before you get all excited, I'm not talking apps like the ones on your phone. Sadly, your calculator won't let you watch TikTok videos in class.

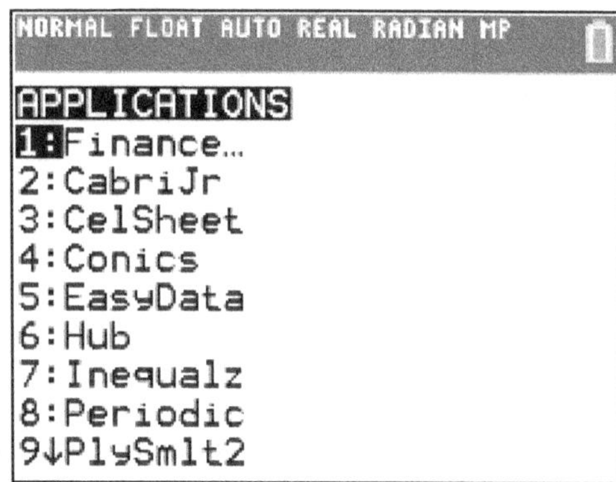

If you need to download an app, you can do so from the Texas Instruments site:

https://education.ti.com/en/downloads

The process is relatively straightforward, but you do need to download some software to a computer.

Using an app is as easy as pressing apps, scrolling to the app you want to use, and pressing enter. Some apps stay on until you turn them off (like Inequalz), and some quit once you quit out of the app.

In many apps, you move forwards and backwards through screens with the graphing buttons.

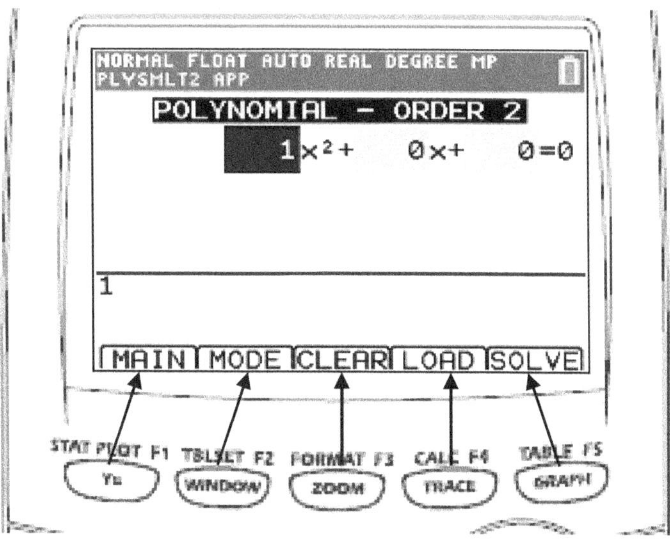

APPendix A: APPS—Conics

Conics allows students to graph four conics: parabolas, circles, ellipses, and hyperbolas. Sometimes, the brute force approach of graphing all five answer choices can work—but it's usually time inefficient.

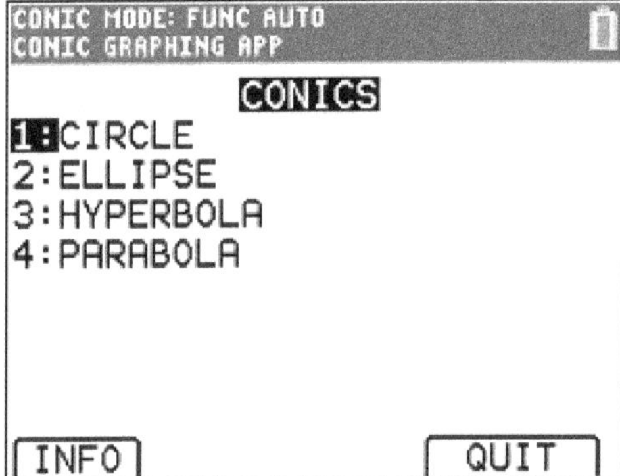

The most beneficial use of conics, in my opinion, is to see the equation that would give you each conic. This can let you rule out multiple answer choices on many ACT conics questions.

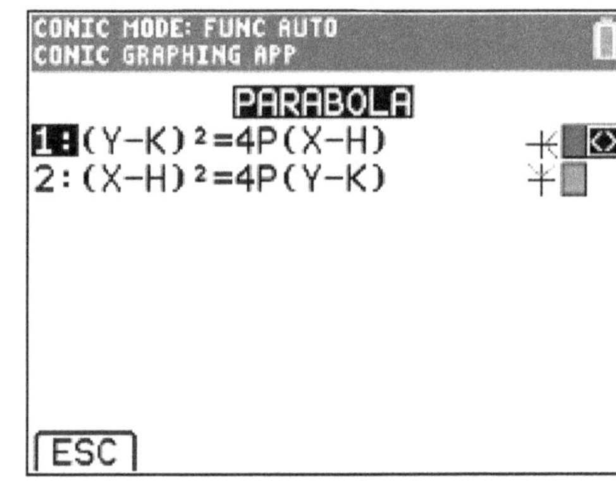

Notice that for parabolas, hyperbolas, and ellipses, you also get the direction of the conic in the red/blue image.

That is, you get to see whether a conic is oriented vertically or horizontally.

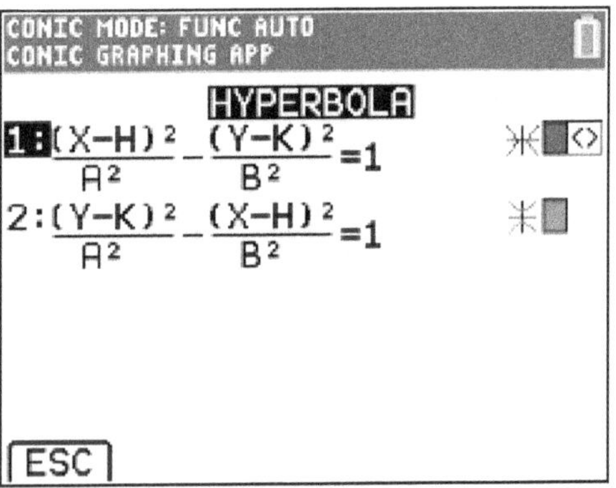

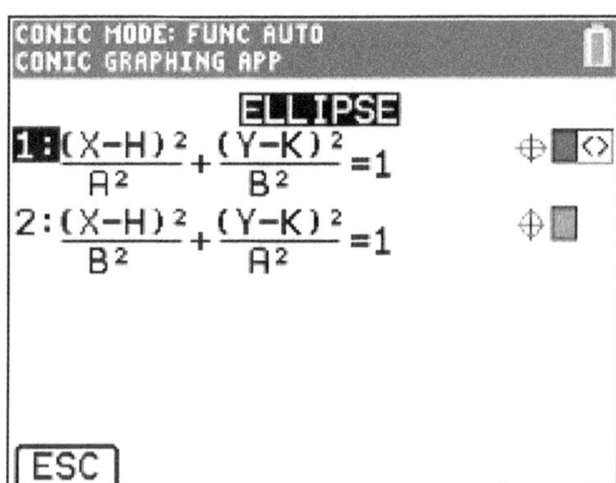

In each of the conics above, (H, K) represents the **center** or **vertex** (for a parabola) of the conic.

For some students who have worked with conics, but forgotten the equations, this can jog a memory.

APPendix A: APPS—Conics

Here's a couple of examples of using the Conics app:

42. One of the following is an equation of the ellipse shown in the standard (x, y) coordinate plane below. Which one?

(Note: the coordinate unit on the x-axis is the same as the coordinate unit on the y-axis.)

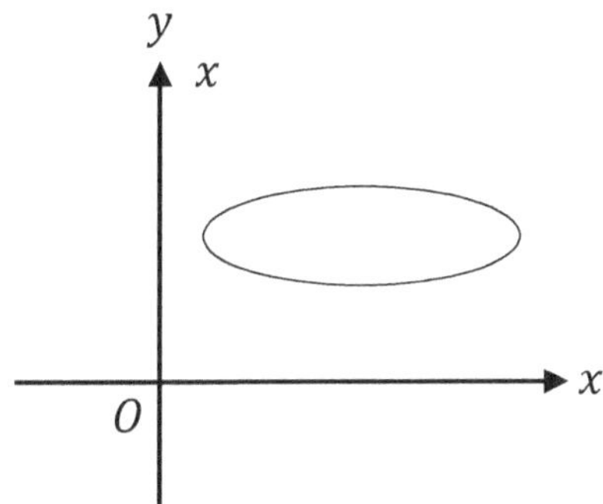

F. $x^2 - y^2 = 36$

G. $(x - 6)^2 + (y - 4)^2 = 36$

H. $\dfrac{(x + 6)^2}{16} - \dfrac{(y + 4)^2}{4} = 1$

J. $\dfrac{(x + 6)^2}{16} + \dfrac{(y + 4)^2}{4} = 1$

K. $\dfrac{(x - 6)^2}{16} + \dfrac{(y - 4)^2}{4} = 1$

Since we know we have an ellipse, we can look up what the formula should be for a horizontal ellipse.

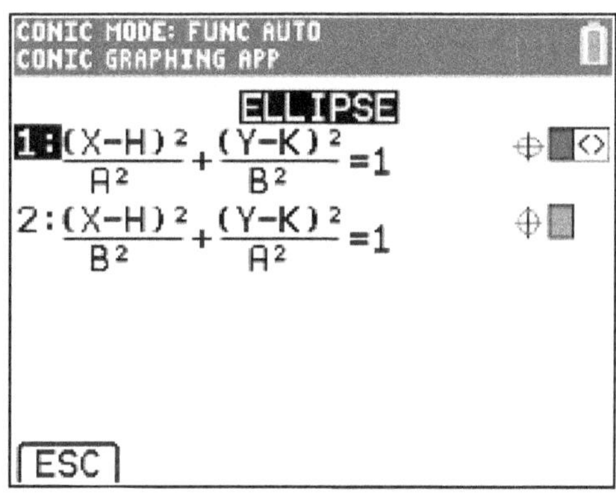

Since answers **F, G,** and **H** do not have the correct forms, you can instantly eliminate them

If you are unsure whether **J** or **K** is correct, you can graph one. I'll graph **J**.

Notice the ellipse ends up in quadrant 3 instead of quadrant 1 like we want. The answer is **K.**

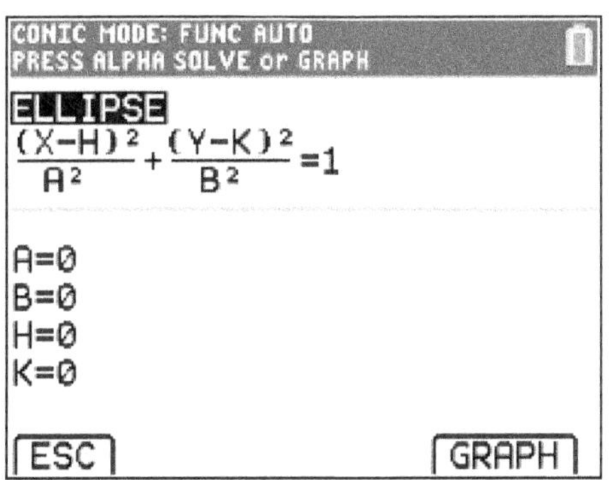

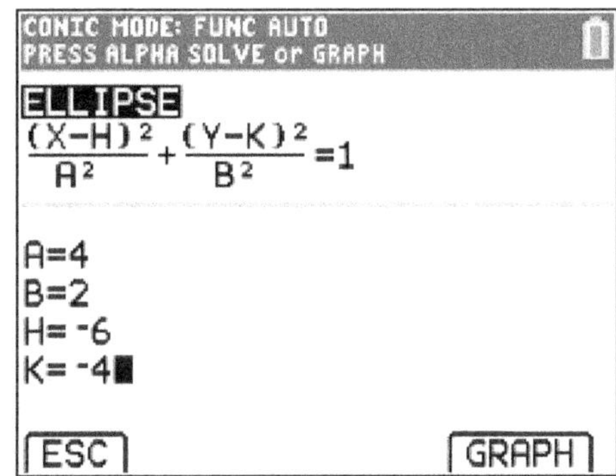

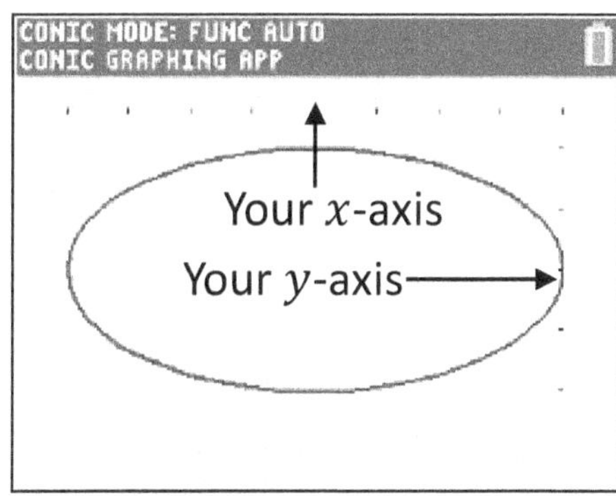

A word of warning—when you put in the A and B value, you are putting in the *square root* of 16 and 4, respectively (hence the 4 and 2). This is because A^2 is in the denominator on the screen and so is 16. Thus, $A^2 = 16$ and $A = 4$.

APPendix A: APPS—Conics

Instead of actually graphing the ellipse, suppose we just wanted to know the center. In the previous example, we can see that the center should be in the first quadrant, so both the x and y should be positive.

1. Put your values into your equation and then press **alpha** **enter**

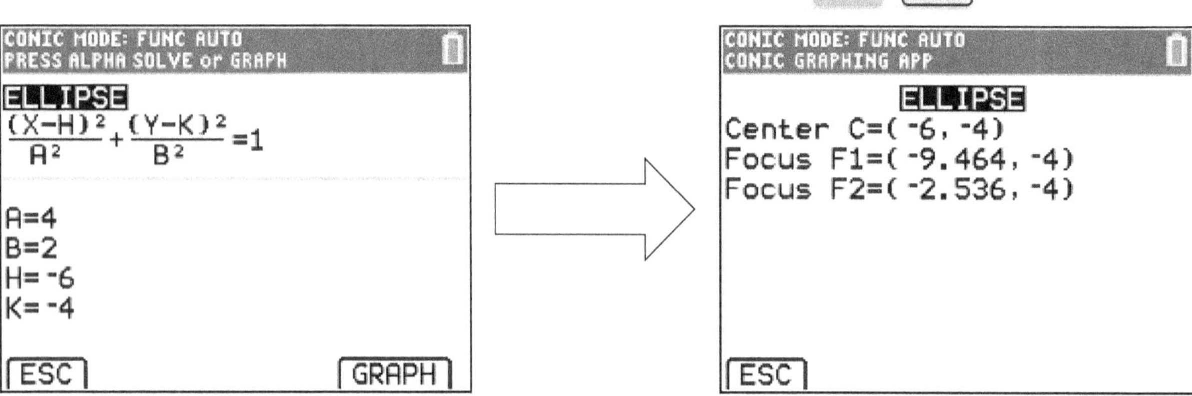

2. Read off the relevant info.

For the previous question, that was enough to eliminate **J** and go with **K** as an answer.

36. A circle in the standard (x, y) coordinate plane has an equation
$$(x - 2)^2 + (y + 1)^2 = 36$$
What are the radius of the circle, in coordinate units, and the coordinates of the center of the circle?

	radius	center
F.	6	$(-2, 1)$
G.	6	$(2, 1)$
H.	18	$(-2, 1)$
J.	18	$(2, 1)$
K.	36	$(2, 1)$

If easier, you can also do this:

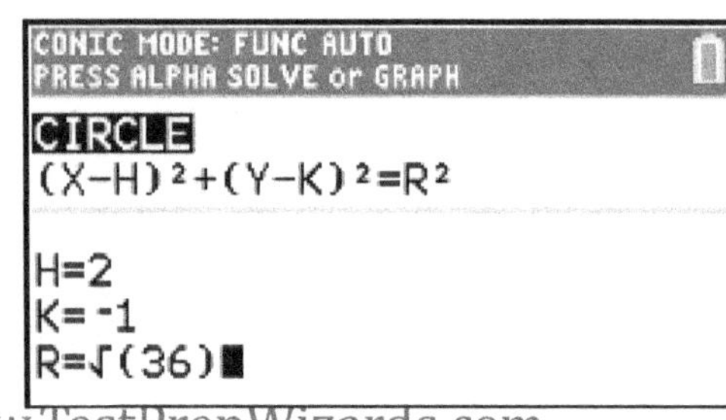

Since we know we have a circle, we can choose the correct form, inputting $H, K,$ and $R.$ Be careful, to put in R, not R^2.

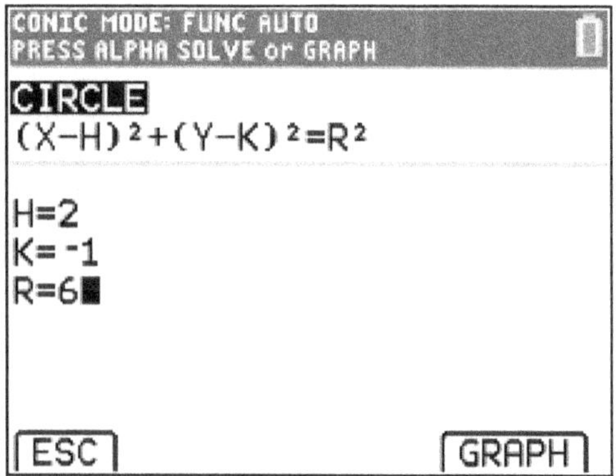

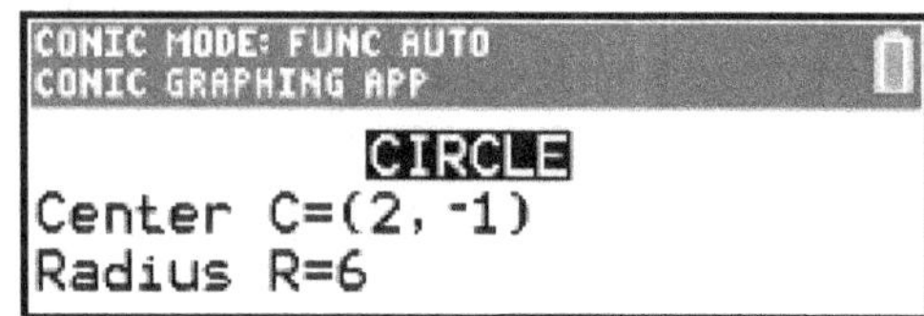

APPendix A: APPS—Inequalz

Inequalz allows you to graph inequalities on your graphing screen as well as find the **solution set**, or region in which all the given inequalities are true, of a number of inequalities.

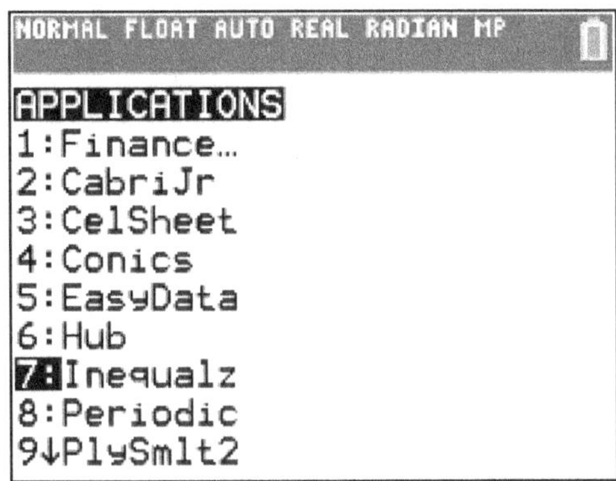 

Once you've activated Inequalz, you'll notice you have some different options for graphing.

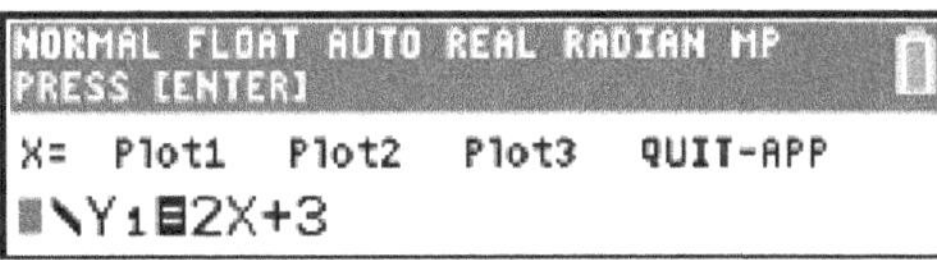

You can move to the left and press enter. This will bring up a screen that allows you to pick what color gets shaded and scroll down to change the type of equality and inequality that gets graphed.

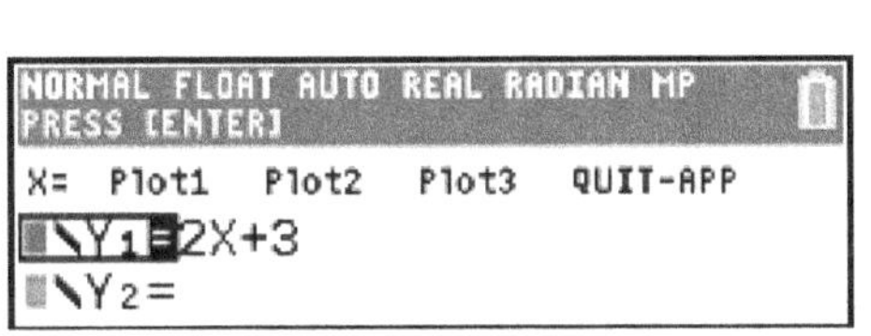 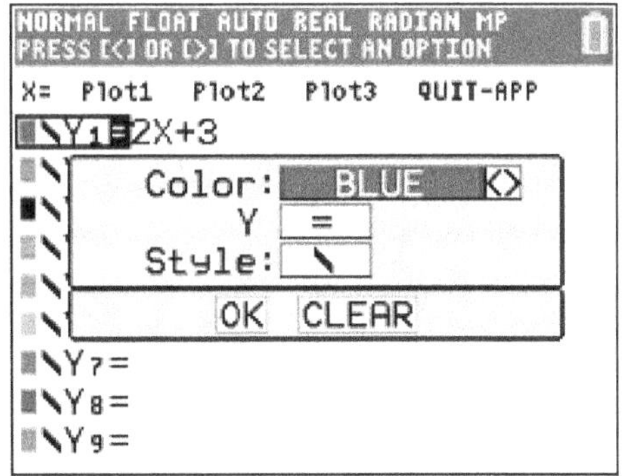 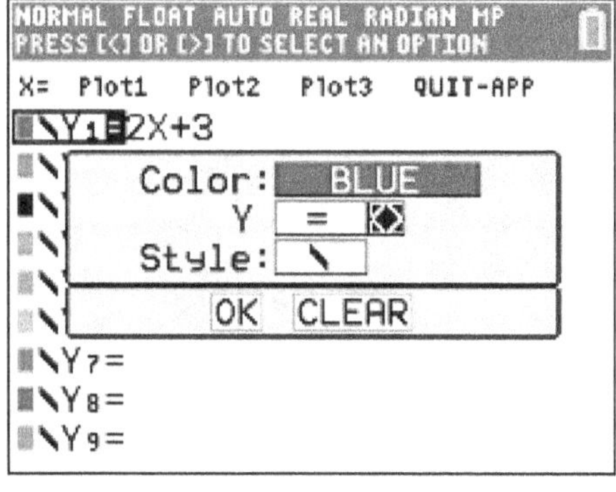

Here are the four inequality options:

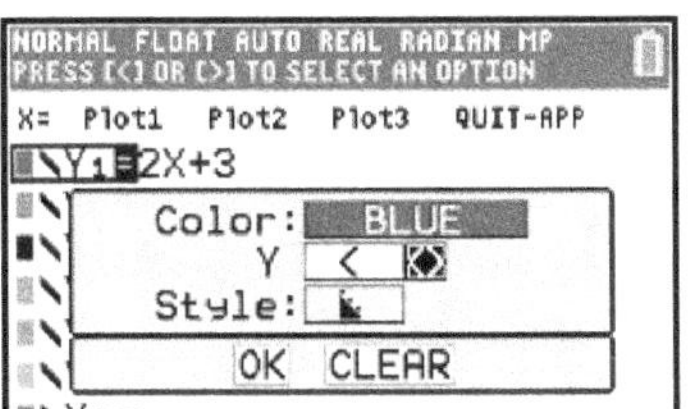 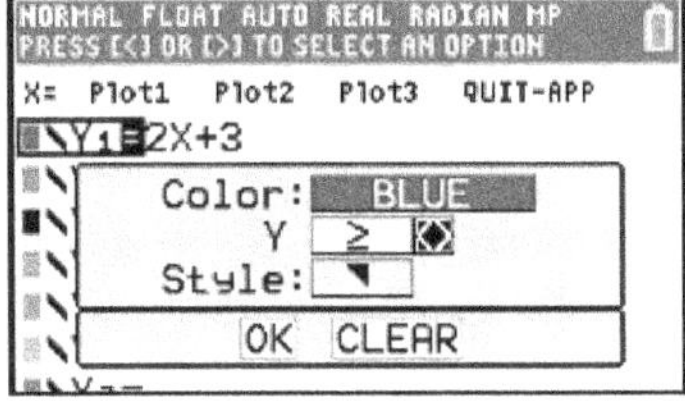  

Notice that the style automatically updates to show you whether your line will be solid or dashed and whether shading will be above or below the line.

APPendix A: APPS—Inequalz

Suppose I choose the option for $\geq$. Once I press OK, I can then graph the function and see the shaded solution space.

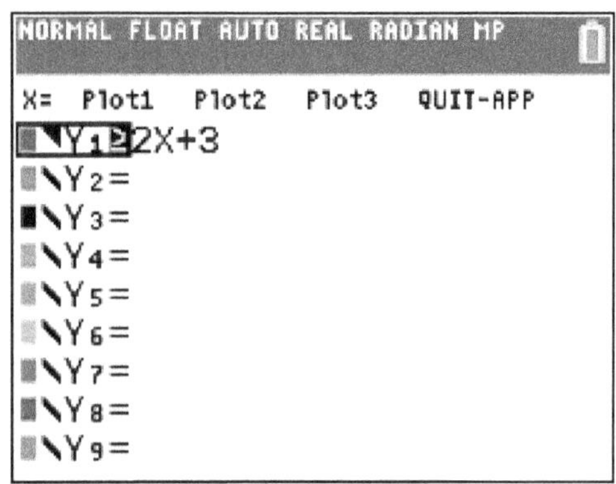

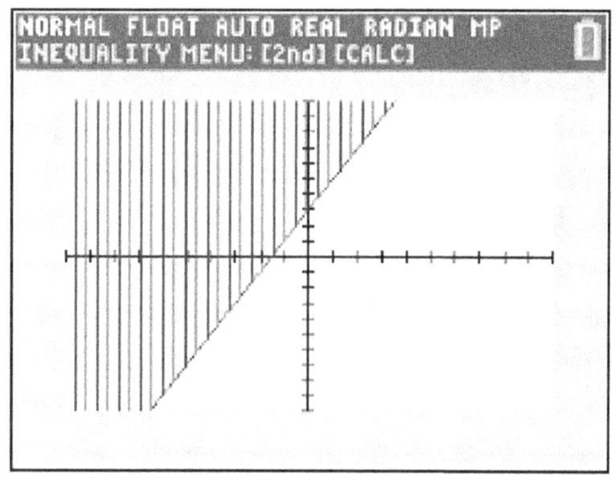

Now that's cool and all, but here's where it's going to go from good to great. The ACT likes graphing system of inequality questions, and these become simple with Inequalz.

Suppose we have to find the solution space for the following system:

$$y \geq 5x - 1$$
$$y < -2x + 8$$
$$y > 3$$

First, press $\boxed{y =}$ and put all three inequalities into Y_1, Y_2, and Y_3 with the correct inequality symbols (remember to scroll left and press $\boxed{\text{enter}}$).

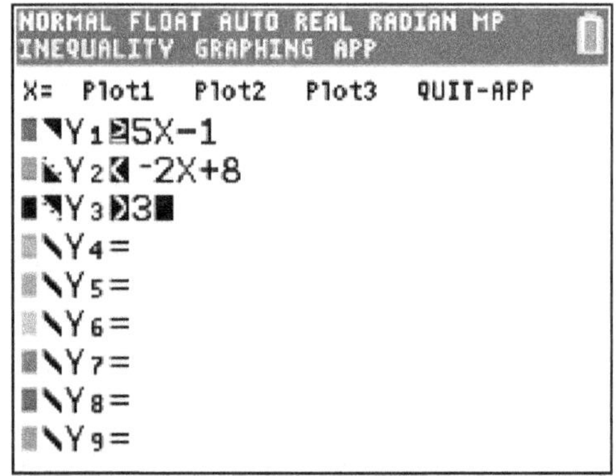

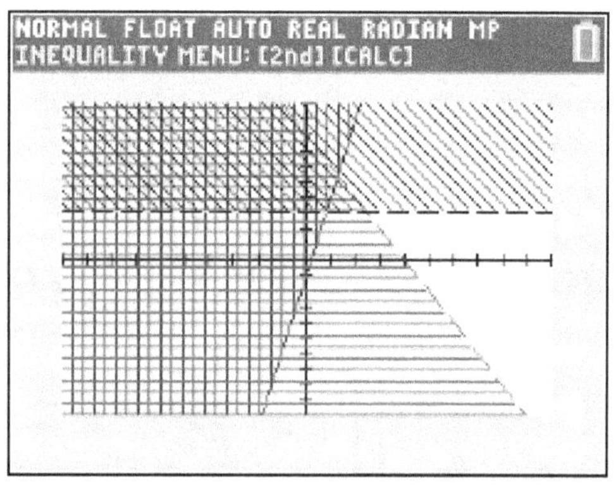

That can help us if we can determine the overlap...wait! Our calculator can determine the overlap. Press:

calc   f4

2nd   trace

APPendix A: APPS—Inequalz

This will access a new menu—scroll to the **INEQUALITY** menu.

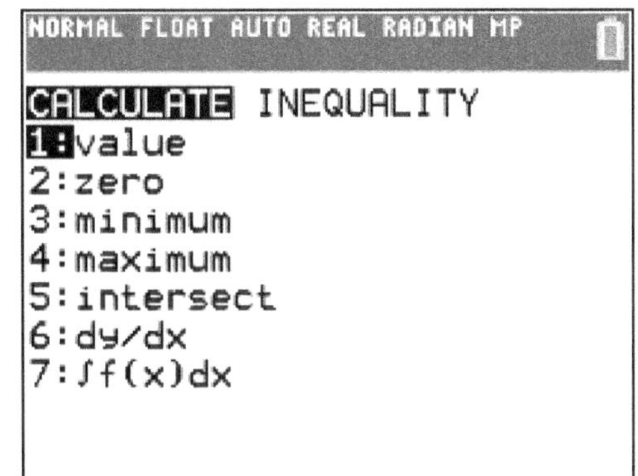
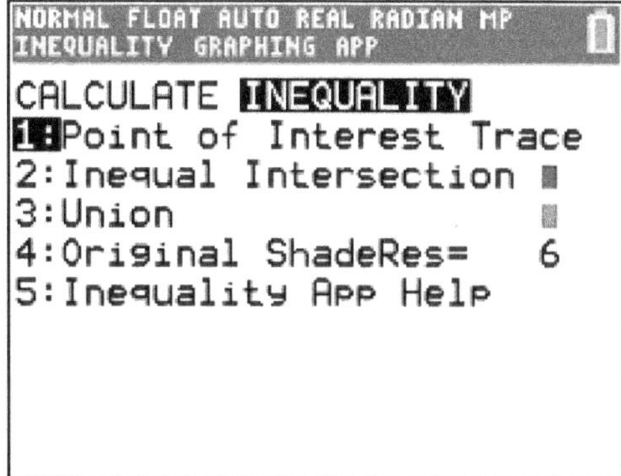

From this menu, choose the second option—**Inequal Intersection**:

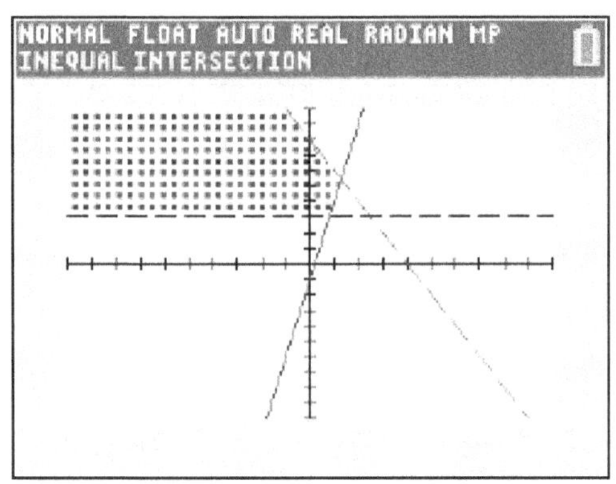

You should see the calculator shade and then remove the parts of the shading that do not fall in the solution space.

Suppose I threw one little monkey wrench into the last system—suppose we now had

$$y \geq 5x - 1$$
$$y < -2x + 8$$
$$y > 3$$
$$x \geq -1$$

We can also graph the vertical line $x \geq -1$. After pressing $\boxed{y =}$, scroll up to the little x in the corner and press $\boxed{\text{enter}}$. Input your inequality and graph, and then find the intersection once more.

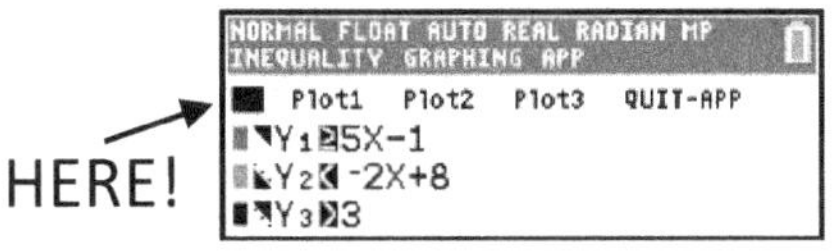

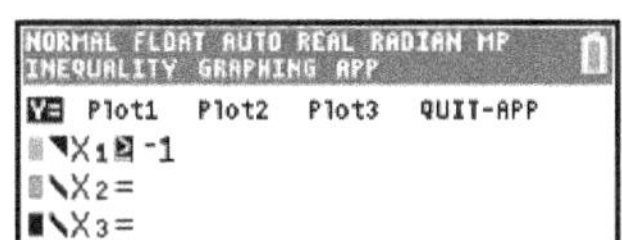
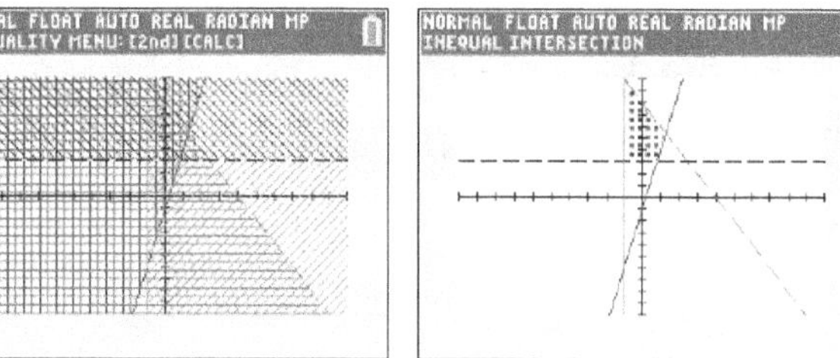

www.TestPrepWizards.com

APPendix A: APPS—PlySmlt2

The last app, PlySmlt2, stands for Polynomial Root Finder and Simultaneous Equation Solver. Basically, it's going to do two things for us:

1. Solve systems of equations.
2. Find the x-intercepts (aka roots, solutions, or zeros of a function) of a polynomial.

To access this app, press $\boxed{\text{apps}}$ and scroll down to PlySmlt2:

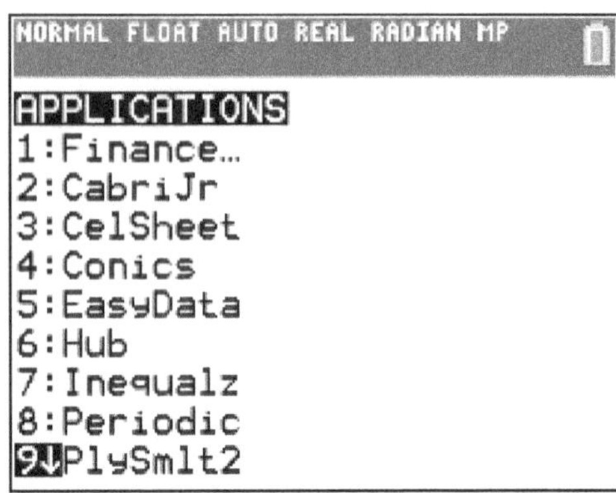
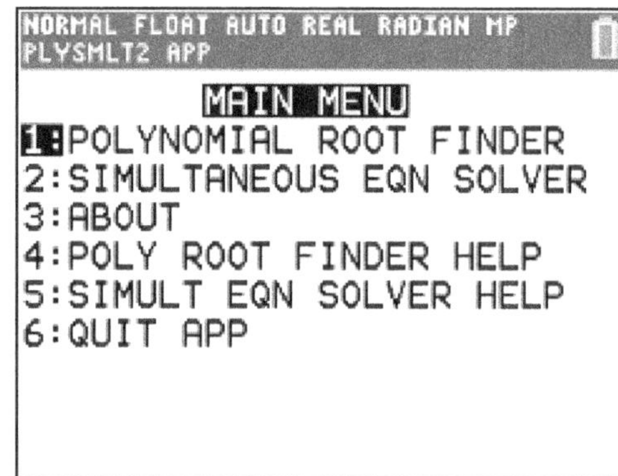

Let's start with the **POLYNOMIAL ROOT FINDER**. When we click on it, we are brought to this screen:

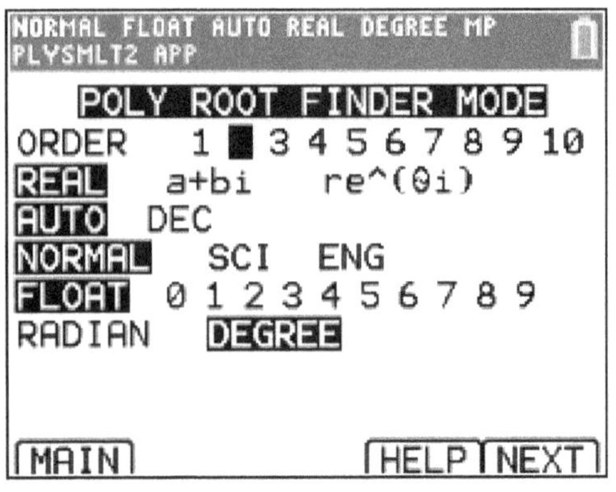

Order is the highest power of the polynomial. In school, we usually refer to it as the **degree**.

REAL will limit answers to the real number system only; $a + bi$ will also include complex solutions—helpful if you see complex numbers in the answer choices!

I recommend leaving AUTO on, if possible. It gives you fraction answers, which tend to show up more than decimal answers on the ACT. Sometimes, you're forced to abide by the calculator's rules depending on order.

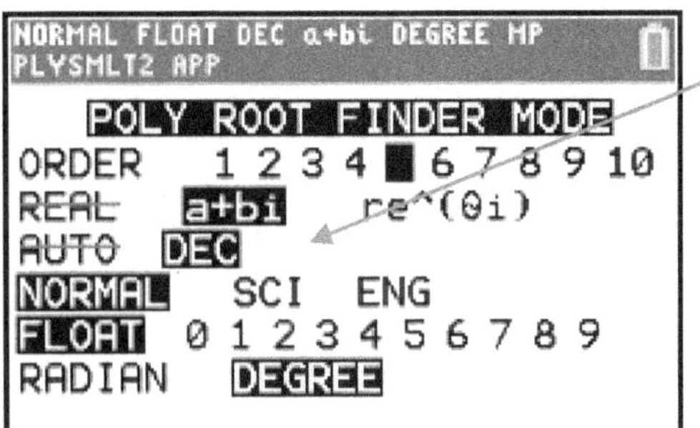

Leave it on NORMAL and DEGREE.

Float is the number of decimal places you want your answers rounded to. Usually 2 or 3 is good enough. If you keep it on FLOAT, you'll get decimals until the calculator runs out of screen space.

www.TestPrepWizards.com

APPendix A: APPS—PlySmlt2

Suppose we are confronted with the following question on the ACT:

32. Which of the following values is a zero of
$f(x) = 2x^3 + 7x^2 - 15x$?

F. -5

G. $-\dfrac{3}{2}$

H. 1

J. 3

K. 5

Here, the order is 3; I'll FLOAT 3 as well.

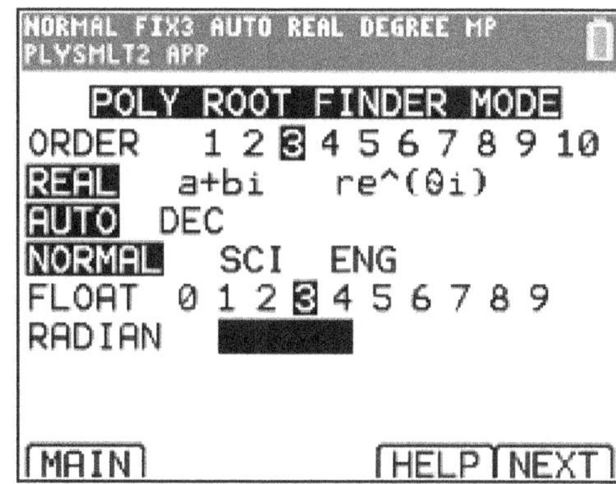

To move to the next screen, press $\boxed{\text{graph}}$. You should get:

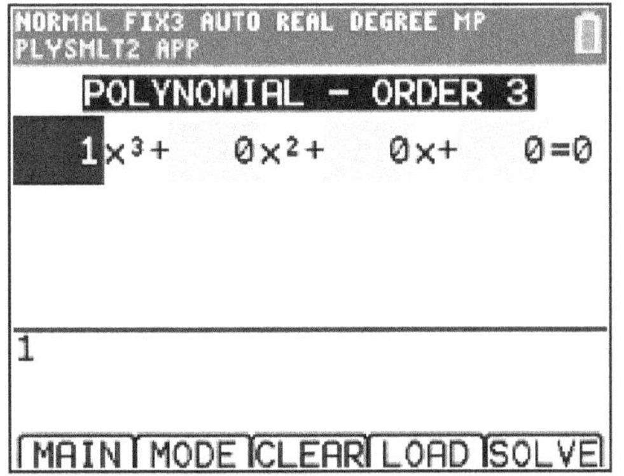

Here, simply plop in the coefficients and change any addition to subtraction as needed.

NOTE: You must have a coefficient or constant for each shaded box. If a term is missing (like our constant in question 32), then make sure you put a 0 in the shaded box.

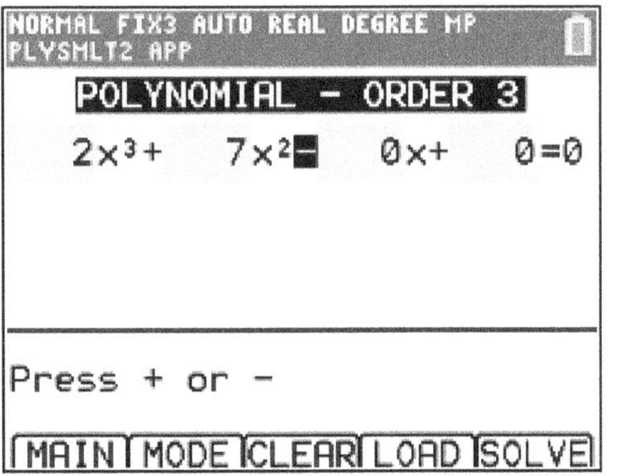

Press $\boxed{\text{enter}}$ as needed to keep proceeding past the notes on the bottom of the screen.

Once you're ready to solve, hit $\boxed{\text{graph}}$ to move to the solution screen.

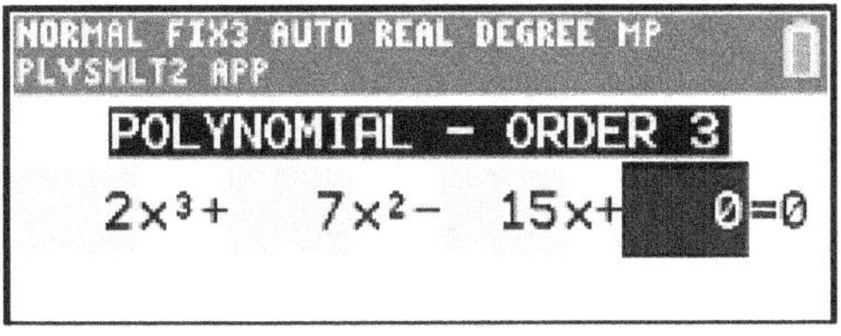

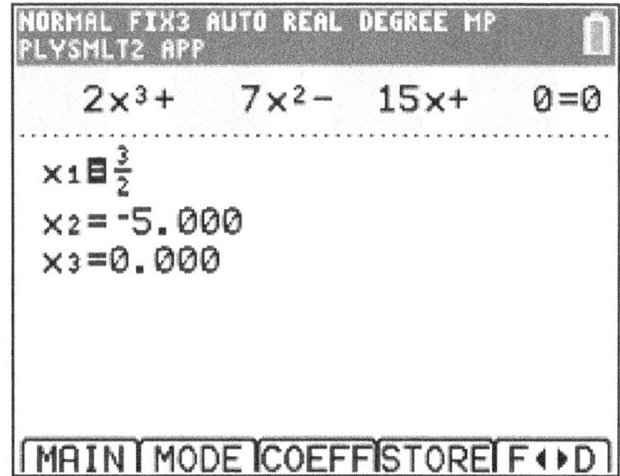

If you need to go back a screen, use the COEFF tab by hitting $\boxed{\text{zoom}}$.

APPendix A: APPS—PlySmlt2

To use the Simultaneous Equation Solver, you first need two equations with two variables. For the ACT, we'll only need to use it for two by two linear systems.

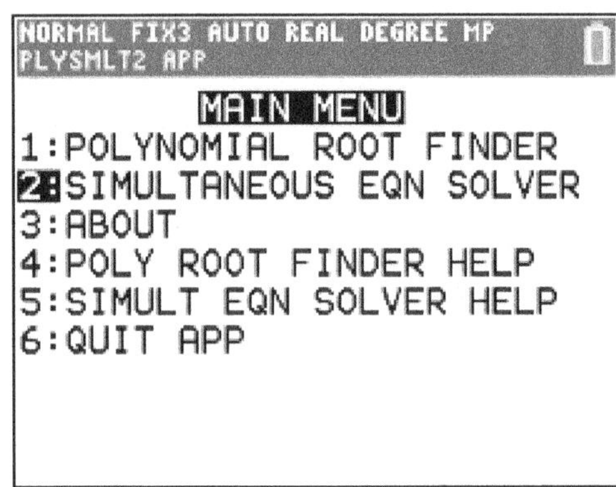
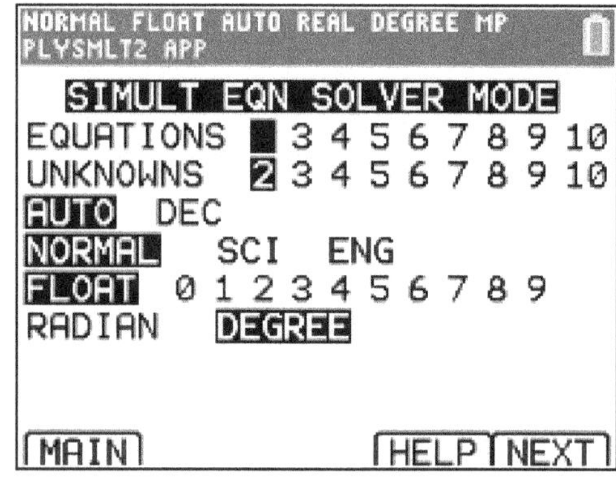

Just like for the Polynomial Root Finder, we'll want to keep our options on AUTO (if possible), NORMAL, DEGREE, and whatever FLOAT seems appropriate.

EQUATIONS is the number of equations—we'll pretty much never need to take it off 2. UNKNOWNS is the number of different variables that are in the equations. We'll also probably never have to take it off 2.

26. What is the solution to the system of equations shown below?

$$3x - 5y = 22$$
$$3x + 3y = 6$$

  F. $(-4, -6)$

  G. $(1, 1)$

  H. $(4, -2)$

  J. $(6, 2)$

  K. $(6, 16)$

From the SIMULT EQN SOLVER MODE window, press ⌗graph⌗ to move to the next screen.

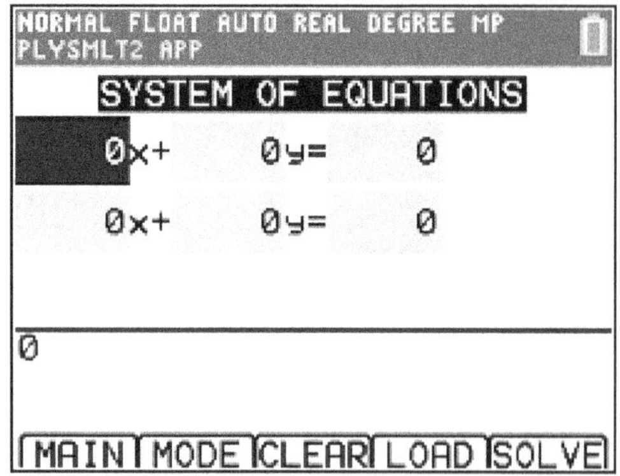

Input your coefficients, pressing ⌗enter⌗ to progress to the addition and subtraction and shaded areas. NOTE: You **MUST** make sure your equations are in standard form, $Ax + By = C$.

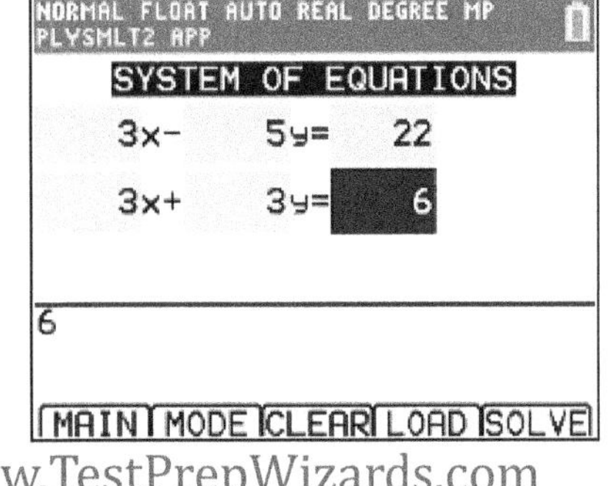

Press ⌗graph⌗

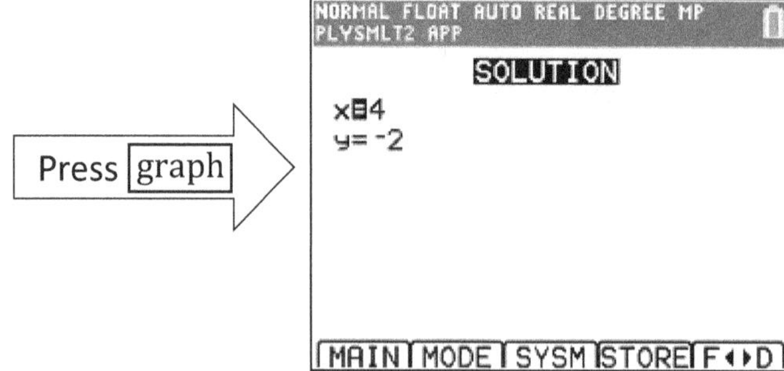

Appendix B: ACT Questions by Topic

In case you have a released ACT from 2019, 2020, or a "Preparing for the ACT," you can practice some of the concepts presented in this manual by using the guides presented in this appendix.

Remember, a calculator is a tool, not a crutch. Being a calculator master will probably not get you as far as being mathematically solid on the ACT. However, true wizards understand when the calculator can aid them come test day!

The next few pages will outline what calculator methods *could* be used to solve certain questions. I apologize in advance if I miss something. Again, just because you *could* use the calculator does not mean you *should* use the calculator; I leave it up to you to determine your individualized best course of action. We also do not discuss questions in which using simple operations to calculate a value (e.g. $8 \times 13 = 104$) is a use of your calculator..

Additionally, I outline how to do questions when they are ready made for the calculator. I do not mention questions that could be solved after some manipulation or by using some test-taking strategy like substituting in your own values.

We will also work to get calculator guides on our website for other released tests.

Stop by www.testprepwizards.com and sign up for updates!

Additionally, we also have a calculator program section on the website above. Programs can take your already cool calculator and level it up to like ∞. Check out the videos explaining how to use the programs and see which ones you'd like to download.

Appendix B: ACT Questions by Topic—Preparing for the ACT (1874F)

Q#	Notes	Q#	Notes	Q#	Notes
1		21		41	
2		22		42	**LOG with FRAC Menu**
3	**NUMERIC SOLVER**	23		43	
4	**YVARS or Storing Variables**	24		44	
5		25	**FRAC Menu with Scientific Notation**	45	
6		26		46	
7		27		47	
8	**FRAC Menu with Storing Variables**	28		48	
9		29		49	
10		30		50	
11	**Storing variables/FRAC Menu**	31		51	
12	**LCM(**	32		52	
13		33		53	
14		34		54	
15	**ABS(**	35		55	
16		36		56	
17		37		57	**MTRX Menu, Det(, and NUMERIC SOLVER**
18		38		58	*i*
19		39		59	
20		40		60	

*Polynomial Root Finder in APPS PlySmlt2
†Simultaneous Equation Solver in APPS PlySmlt2
‡Conics in APPS Conics

A student with a 21 on this ACT (30 correct) who now got each of these 10 calculator questions would end up with a 26 on this ACT.

www.TestPrepWizards.com

Appendix B: ACT Questions by Topic—Preparing for the ACT (1572C)

Q#	Notes	Q#	Notes	Q#	Notes
1		21		41	
2	1-VAR STATS (mean)	22		42	YVARS or Storing Variables
3	FRAC Menu with Mixed Numbers	23		43	
4		24		44	
5	YVARS or Storing Variables	25		45	
6		26		46	
7		27		47	
8		28		48	FRAC Menu
9		29	i	49	
10	1-VAR STATS (median)	30		50	
11		31		51	
12		32	FRAC Menu	52	
13		33		53	
14		34		54	
15		35		55	
16		36		56	
17		37	1-VAR STATS (mean & median)	57	
18		38		58	
19	Scientific Notation	39		59	
20		40		60	

*Polynomial Root Finder in APPS PlySmlt2
†Simultaneous Equation Solver in APPS PlySmlt2
‡Conics in APPS Conics

A student with a 21 on this ACT (30 correct) who now got each of these 10 calculator questions would end up with a 26 on this ACT.

Appendix B: ACT Questions by Topic—B04 April 2019

Q#	Notes	Q#	Notes	Q#	Notes
1	**NUMERIC SOLVER**	21		41	
2		22		42	**LOGBASE/NUMERIC SOLVER**
3		23		43	
4		24		44	
5		25		45	
6		26	**1-VAR STATS (median)**	46	
7	**FRAC Menu**	27		47	
8		28		48	
9		29		49	
10		30	**MTRX Menu**	50	
11	**Storing variables/FRAC Menu**	31		51	
12	**LCM(**	32	**Simultaneous EQN Solver†**	52	
13		33		53	
14		34		54	
15		35		55	**REMAINDER**
16	**NUMERIC SOLVER/Root Finder***	36		56	**Conics‡**
17		37		57	
18	**FRAC Menu**	38		58	
19		39		59	
20		40	**YVARS**	60	

*Polynomial Root Finder in APPS PlySmlt2
†Simultaneous Equation Solver in APPS PlySmlt2
‡Conics in APPS Conics

A student with a 21 on this ACT (30 correct) who now got each of these 13 calculator questions would end up with a 28 on this ACT.

Appendix B: ACT Questions by Topic—Z15 April 2019

Q#	Notes	Q#	Notes	Q#	Notes
1	**Storing Variables**	21		41	
2		22		42	
3		23		43	
4		24		44	
5		25		45	**1-VAR STATS (frequency table)**
6	**ABS(**	26		46	
7		27		47	
8		28		48	
9	**FRAC Menu**	29		49	
10	**NUMERIC SOLVER**	30	**FRAC Menu**	50	**Roots**
11	**Storing Variables/YVARS**	31		51	**MTRX Menu**
12		32		52	
13		33		53	
14		34		54	
15	**FRAC Menu**	35	**FRAC Menu**	55	
16		36		56	**Factorials**
17		37	**FRAC Menu**	57	
18		38		58	**MTRX Determinant**
19		39	**LCM(**	59	**NUMERIC SOLVER/Root Finder***
20		40		60	

*Polynomial Root Finder in APPS PlySmlt2
†Simultaneous Equation Solver in APPS PlySmlt2
‡Conics in APPS Conics

A student with a 21 on this ACT (30 correct) who now got each of these 16 calculator questions would end up with a 27 on this ACT.

Appendix B: ACT Questions by Topic—B02 June 2019

Q#	Notes	Q#	Notes	Q#	Notes
1		21		41	
2	**Storing Variables**	22		42	**Conics‡**
3		23	**Storing Variables/YVARS**	43	
4	**NUMERIC SOLVER/FRAC Menu**	24		44	**NUMERIC SOLVER (find a)**
5		25	**Storing Variables/YVARS**	45	
6		26		46	**FRAC Menu**
7		27		47	
8		28	**Roots**	48	
9		29		49	**NUMERIC SOLVER/Root Finder***
10		30		50	
11		31		51	
12	**Simultaneous EQN Solver†**	32		52	
13		33		53	
14	**FRAC Menu/ABS(**	34		54	
15		35		55	**Inequalz (Kind of)**
16		36		56	
17		37	**1-VAR STATS (frequency table)**	57	
18		38	**FRAC Menu**	58	**1-VAR STATS (frequency table)**
19		39		59	
20		40		60	**MTRX Menu**

*Polynomial Root Finder in APPS PlySmlt2
†Simultaneous Equation Solver in APPS PlySmlt2
‡Conics in APPS Conics

A student with a 22 on this ACT (30 correct) who now got each of these 16 calculator questions would end up with a 29 on this ACT.

Appendix B: ACT Questions by Topic—C03 December 2019

Q#	Notes	Q#	Notes	Q#	Notes
1	**Storing Variables**	21		41	
2		22		42	
3		23		43	
4		24		44	
5	**Storing Variables**	25		45	
6		26		46	
7		27		47	
8		28	**NUMERIC SOLVER**	48	
9		29		49	
10		30		50	
11		31		51	
12		32		52	
13		33		53	**Conics‡**
14		34		54	
15	**LCM(**	35		55	
16		36		56	
17		37		57	**REMAINDER**
18	**NUMERIC SOLVER/FRAC Menu**	38		58	
19	**1-VAR STATS (Average)**	39	**FRAC Menu**	59	*i*
20		40	**REMAINDER**	60	

*Polynomial Root Finder in APPS PlySmlt2
†Simultaneous Equation Solver in APPS PlySmlt2
‡Conics in APPS Conics

A student with a 20 on this ACT (30 correct) who now got each of these 11 calculator questions would end up with a 26 on this ACT.

Appendix B: ACT Questions by Topic—C02 June 2020

Q#	Notes	Q#	Notes	Q#	Notes
1	GCD(	21		41	LOGBASE/NUMERIC SOLVER
2		22		42	
3		23		43	
4		24		44	
5		25		45	
6		26		46	
7		27		47	Conics‡
8		28		48	
9	FRAC Menu	29		49	
10		30		50	
11		31		51	
12	Storing Variables/YVARS	32		52	
13	Storing Variables/YVARS	33	Storing Variables/YVARS	53	
14		34		54	
15		35		55	
16	ABS(	36		56	i
17		37		57	
18	1-VAR STATS (Average, Median)	38		58	
19		39		59	
20		40		60	

*Polynomial Root Finder in APPS PlySmlt2
†Simultaneous Equation Solver in APPS PlySmlt2
‡Conics in APPS Conics

A student with a 21 on this ACT (30 correct) who now got each of these 10 calculator questions would end up with a 26 on this ACT.

Q#	Notes	Q#	Notes	Q#	Notes
1		21		41	**FRAC Menu and Exponents**
2		22		42	**LOGBASE/NUMERIC SOLVER**
3	**GCD(**	23		43	
4	**NUMERIC SOLVER**	24		44	**LCM(**
5		25		45	
6		26		46	
7		27		47	
8		28		48	
9	**NUMERIC SOLVER**	29		49	
10		30	**MTRX Menu**	50	
11	**FRAC Menu**	31		51	
12		32		52	
13		33		53	**NUMERIC SOLVER**
14		34		54	
15		35		55	
16	**FRAC Menu**	36		56	
17		37		57	**Factorials**
18		38		58	
19		39		59	
20		40		60	

*Polynomial Root Finder in APPS PlySmlt2
†Simultaneous Equation Solver in APPS PlySmlt2
‡Conics in APPS Conics

A student with a 22 on this ACT (30 correct) who now got each of these 11 calculator questions would end up with a 27 on this ACT.